Into I

A Marine Sniper's War

Joe Chamblin

with Milo Afong

ISBN -10:151173289X

ISBN-13: 978-1511732895

Cover Photo

The cover photo is Sgt. Mark A. Bradley over looking the valley of Mt. Musa Quelah, Afghanistan. He was a member of Reaper 2. The photo was taken in May, a month before he was wounded on June 3, 2011. He died of his wounds at Bethesda Naval Hospital on June 16, 2011, surrounded by his family. Sgt. Bradley was born July 7, 1985, he was 25 years old. His home was in Clayton, NC.

DEDICATION

Dedicated to my brother Scout Snipers
and fellow Marines who fought the good fight.

ACKNOWLEDGMENTS

I'd like to thank my Marine Brother, Milo Afong for his untiring help in writing this book with me. Also Ed Kugler for raising funds and making this book happen, Robert Fraser for his work in editing this book and Steve Alexander for his beautiful cover design. I would be remiss if I didn't thank the nearly 300 donors who helped our story to be told by donating during our Kickstarter Campaign. Last but certainly not last I would like to thank my family and friends for their loyalty and support throughout it all.

CONTENTS

Acknowledgments i

Foreword 1

1 The Beginning of the End 5

2 Into the Brotherhood 31

3 Joining the Fight 43

4 Hunter of Gunmen 67

5 School Trained 79

6 Teaching to Fighting 109

7 The Fray 125

8 Mid-Deployment 143

9 Our Loss 159

10 Heating Up 171

11 The Day of Infamy 181

12 Sniper Operations 195

13 Coming Home 207

About the Author 215

Joe Chamblin

FOREWORD

Marine Scout Snipers have proven to be extremely effective against insurgent forces. However, in a war in which our country focused on nation building, the use of snipers may seem politically incorrect. For some, the term "sniper" itself sounds like a dirty word, evoking images of bloodthirsty barbarians indiscriminately killing people for personal pleasure.

But snipers, in fact, hold human life in high regard and are more conscious about the decision to take lives than other methods in war. While pilots drop smart bombs on entire buildings, and machine gunners suppress targets at 700 rounds a minute, snipers are different. We take one precise shot at a time, and, at the place of our choosing. We can eliminate a designated target in crowded streets or marketplaces while preserving the life of the innocent. Creating security without collateral damage is key to winning the hearts and minds of people, and while politicians in Washington will never admit it, snipers are the perfect solution to this insurgency.

Snipers in a war zone endure many hardships. Often, in order to accomplish our task undetected, we are required to infiltrate in the early morning hours, long before dawn. To do so, it takes noise and light discipline. More often than not, sleeping and eating is replaced with observing and reporting. In order to accomplish our mission, we have to make physical sacrifices.

As snipers, we've accepted the possibility of death, and if we die, our bodies may never be returned. Perhaps most importantly, we sacrifice our mental sanity in order to accomplish our tasks. Imagine observing a specific building or road junction for days at a time, in the hopes that even one insurgent may present himself. We're looking to save lives. The insurgent may be placing an IED (Improvised Explosive Device) or setting up to shoot at ground units. You've been sitting there for hours, maybe days, and you have a 30 second window to engage the enemy. A small space to distinguish between friend from foe. Thirty seconds!

The difference between an insurgent and a civilian is often indistinguishable. When fighting a war of insurgents, who hide amongst the general public, an 'insurgent' burying a roadside bomb may very well turn out to be an otherwise unsuspecting farmer digging a water furrow. We must rely on instinct, detecting the slightest nuances in order to tip us off. If we fail, we know that our mistake could lead to one of our brothers being harmed. It's an incredible task for a young man to undertake, knowing that the slightest lapse in judgment could be the mistake that ends our life or that of our brothers.

Into Infamy - A Marine Sniper's War, is a book written by a fellow Marine, Joe Chamblin. He tells the compelling story of real life Marines and their war against terrorism. *Into Infamy* is a story of brotherhood, death, life, love, hate, and fear. Far too few people experience or comprehend what our warriors endure. Joe's group has endured much. From the high of breakfast with the Commandant for their accomplishments to the low of a YouTube video that destroyed lives and careers.

My Foreword is an attempt to open the eyes of the public to the truth about my fellow warriors and me. The men, who not only participated in the wars but fought them face-to-face with the enemy.

J. D.
USMC Scout/Sniper

"When your time comes to die, be not like those whose hearts are filled with fear of death, so that when their time comes they weep and pray for a little more time to live their lives over again in a different way. Sing your death song, and die like a hero going home."

Tecumseh
Shawnee War Chief

1 THE BEGINNING OF THE END

The Final Shot

"Guys, this is it. Once we finish this one, we're done. We have intel that the High-Value Individual (HVI), our target, Mr. Khar, will be at our objective," I said. "Let's go up there, get him, and make these fuckers pay. Be staged and ready to move at 2000 hours."

The men knew what to do. By now, we'd been in this shit hole known as Helmand Province for nearly seven months, and our time to rotate home was almost up, but we weren't home yet. I wasn't one to count my blessings early, and it was my job to make sure our other snipers didn't either.

With less than a month left in the country, our teams needed to execute one last mission. As the sniper platoon commander, part of my job meant sitting in on and assisting with the planning of sniper operations for the battalion. It took a few days to hammer out the details for this, our final op.

The disruption operation called for killing or capturing the elusive Mr. Khar. He'd held a spot on our shit list for quite awhile. A few months earlier, during a reconnaissance mission, one of our teams, Reaper Two, had tracked and photographed him and his goons in a remote valley, but we weren't able to get him.

This time we planned to send three sniper teams, with attachments, and me to infiltrate the heavily defended Taliban valley. We wanted to lure the enemy out. We'd finish them off using a tactic that we'd refined over the past few months. The mission was part of our ultimate goal, to in make a lasting impact in that area by cutting off the snake's head. We targeted commanders and other high-value individuals.

There were a few potential snags we had to work out. In this particular valley, no units had been as far north as we planned to go on this operation. We didn't know exactly what to expect. A CJSOTF (Combined Joint Special Operations Task Force) team had unsuccessfully attempted to apprehend a Taliban commander in the valley a month prior. Some of our snipers were able to watch the wrath brought on by the AC-130 Specter gunships during the fighting. Their arsenal pummeled the valley, igniting a sensational mix of explosions. But because they'd taken an ass whuppin', the enemy would most likely be on high alert.

Entering the valley was another complication. The only reasonable route was from the south, which enemy spotters kept eyes on at all times. At the slightest whiff of intruders, enemy commanders deployed their fighters to preplanned positions along what they conceived would be the most anticipated route. They also constructed a linear defense-in-depth, which was maneuverable, except that doing so at night meant a good chance of losing your legs. Taliban weren't the bravest or smartest fighters, but those dirt squirrels were pretty good at planting IEDs and booby traps.

In the end, we reverted to sniper doctrine. We planned to take the least traveled, most difficult route into the valley by traversing the open desert and button hooking into the valley on foot over the mountains from the north.

I heard a few grumbles about the mission since we were so close to going home. I hated Afghanistan too but loved my job. I was a Marine Sniper running operations from an outpost deep in enemy territory. I had played 'war games' as a kid, except now it was real and had been real for the last ten years of my life.

In that time, I'd become fortunate enough to learn every aspect of Marine sniper operations. From radio operator to point man, team leader to chief scout, and even teaching as a Scout/Sniper Instructor. As with most jobs, however, the longer you stay in the Corps, the farther you get from the fun, and on this deployment, I found myself commanding the sniper platoon.

Snipers are alpha males in every sense of the word. That said, you could only lead them if they respect you enough to follow. Gaining respect boils down to trust, and my men trusted that I would be right beside them the entire time, never asking them to do something I hadn't already done or wouldn't do with them.

They trusted that I would do my job. The basics of that meant keeping them supplied, keeping the battalion informed on sniper operations and coordinating all sniper activity within the battalion. Usually, a commissioned officer fills the billet, not a Staff Sergeant, and usually the platoon commander doesn't take a sniper rifle out on missions. But I wasn't ready to give that up just yet. Occasionally, I had to let the boys know that this old man could still shoot.

To start the mission, we piled into armored vehicles and slipped off base after dark. With attachments, the total size of our force was just over thirty. Since 2010, NATO and ISAF (International Security Assistance Force) mandated size requirements for troops leaving bases. That forced us to operate in eight-man sniper teams. It was somewhat of a handicap, as it made for a bigger footprint, but being Marines we adapted. We formed our teams with four school-trained snipers and four pre-selected infantryman, which proved to work just fine. In fact, worked to our advantage many times.

We chose to travel a known supply route and insert from there. Even if someone were watching, they wouldn't be suspicious of vehicles stopping, and it was so dark they couldn't see us being dropped. The plan seemed good on paper, but hitting the ground running was a different story.

Along the way, we ran into Murphy and his law, and one of the trucks broke down. If the drivers couldn't get it up and running, and we couldn't get into position before BMNT (Beginning of Morning Nautical Twilight) or day break, the mission would be scratched. Fortunately, they made it work and reached the drop off point, but with no time to spare.

It was pitch black as Josh Seiple and his team, Reaper Five, took point and led us into the valley. Josh grew up a farm boy like me and was about as solid a man as you could find. He'd seen combat twice before in Iraq. I felt for him, knowing that he had spent seven years just trying to get a slot to Sniper School. When he finally did, he passed. No problem. He was meticulous in his planning, and I'd watched him mature into a valued leader in the platoon over the deployment.

As we moved towards the objective, it was a ball buster. We patrolled up and down ridge lines, through Wadis, and over steep rugged peaks, back down into the flatlands, and climbed another jagged ridge. A couple hours later, in sweat-soaked cammies, we approached our FFPs (Final Firing Positions) and separated into three groups. Reaper Five went northwest to cover a predicted avenue of approach. They would also cover our movement out. They intended to occupy a compound at the base of the valley, but as they approached, they noticed flashlights inside. Josh decided to move his team onto a ridge line instead.

I recruited the leader of Reaper Four, Rob Richards, to join our platoon. Rob attended Quantico Sniper School when I instructed there and had previously deployed with Sixth Marines to Garmsir and Marjah. He'd been hit and seriously injured by an IED there. He was tough and recovered from his injuries, but still carried shrapnel in his body. Rob led Reaper Four to the south. They had also planned to take a compound but moved onto a ridge, once they realized that their visibility was extremely limited from that structure.

Nate Hervey was Reaper Two's team leader. His team, a few attachments, and I stayed central on the ridge expecting the spot to have a prime view of the valley. At six foot three inches of muscles and tattoos, Nate looked menacing. At a glance, you might think he was a meathead, which would be a big mistake. He was one of the most intelligent and well-rounded snipers around. He came to the platoon highly recommended from other sniper instructors I knew.

In position, two snipers would observe while others held security, and others arranged the hide site.

"Anything?" I asked our radio attachment, who was able to monitor enemy radio traffic.

"Negative Staff Sergeant," he replied. That was good, the bad guys didn't know we were here.

There was nothing left for me to do except wait until daybreak; that's when all the action would start. I decided to get some shuteye and hoped the pain in my body would subside.

The patrol was exhausting, but more so, seven months of constant combat operations had taken its toll on my body. I knew the men also felt it. Most of them had lost weight since arriving. The deployments always affected us physically. We arrived fit and healthy, but gradually wore down.

My injuries were another problem. Most thirty-four-year-olds in the infantry and snipers no less had injuries. I'd had back surgery for a herniated disk, and long patrols always aggravated it. To top it off, a throbbing migraine left me feeling like I'd a sledgehammer had slammed through my head.

With all teams in place, the first phase of our plan was complete. We were firmly in enemy held terrain, and from our separate locations, we could defend ourselves and dictate the enemy's movement. Now all we needed was for Mr. Khar and his fighters to show themselves.

Before I dozed off I asked Doc, our Corpsman, for some Tylenol. I hoped it would help to start a short nap. I held my rifle, curled into a ball, and dozed off. I figured someone would wake me up before the action started. I was wrong.

A few hundred meters to our southeast, Rob's team had found an ideal vantage point. They hid just behind the crest of a ridge and used periscopes to observe the area. As they did, the Fajr or dawn prayer echoed throughout the valley.

Suddenly, a few men gathered near a compound 250 meters away. Four quickly turned to fourteen, and they all carried Soviet block weapons. Rob's team intercepted their handheld ICOM radio chatter, and the Terp (interpreter) excitedly spoke up.

"This is them; this is who you want!" exclaimed the Terp.

"They're doing radio checks for the positions throughout the valley and getting a head count."

That was all the information we needed to engage.

"Get team two on the radio for a coordinated shot," said Rob.

He grabbed the M240B machine gun because it increased his chances of killing more in the first volley. At roughly 200 meters, with the angle, he would rain down lead on them. His ATL (Assistant Team Leader) reached for the M40A5, a Marine sniper's primary bolt-action rifle.

Team two was on alert. Nate assigned his snipers to monitor the compound and the area where Rob has caught site of the men gathering. That's where we expected to find Mr. Khar. The plan was to let as many insurgents gather as possible so that they'd have more targets to ambush. That's what happened.

"Let's initiate contact," Nate calmly relayed over the radio.

Within minutes, both teams had set priorities on multiple targets and waited for the 'countdown to fire'.

Nate lay behind his M40A5 with the scope already adjusted to the men's position. They were roughly 700 meters away. He sighted his crosshairs on a man wearing black garb and standing central in the group with a handheld radio. He seemed to be directing the action. The enemy fighters had no clue that two sniper teams were about to trap them in an L-shaped ambush.

With our teams set, our comm guy counted down on the net: Five, four, three, on two, the scoped rifles opened up, on one, the valley erupted with machine gun fire. Rob held his sights low at the center of the group knowing that his rounds would naturally rise as he squeezed the trigger. He fired nearly two hundred rounds when the shooting started.

Nate calmed his breathing. Training kicked in, as he honed his senses. He applied the fundamentals. Nothing mystical, nothing magical, it was just the fundamentals of shooting. He and another sniper sent their first round at the director, killing him on the spot.

Next to him, five or six other fighters instantly dropped. The rest scattered like roaches.

The gunfire scared the shit out of me. I woke up and immediately crawled to the firing line to check the situation.

"Thanks for waking me up first," I yelled.

"Dude, I'm sorry! Shit happened so fast I didn't have time," Nate replied with a chuckle.

From our position, we had clear visibility of the entire area. As it is in Afghanistan, mud-walled compounds spread across the valley floor. Crop fields stretched to the edges of dirt walkways and roads. Tree lines occasionally skirted the edges of canals and wadis.

I found the ambush site in my scope. The bodies lay in pools of blood. Their weapons sat close. The deaths and our shooting caused enemy radio traffic to jump. We stirred the hornet's nest and thrown a bloody first punch, but it was only a matter of time before the enemy would maneuver on us.

Next to me, Nate found more targets. Rob and team four were relentless and chewed up a small team trying to regroup. Two men, assuming they were safe from team four, found cover behind a wall. Then found themselves directly in the crosshairs of Nate.

He fired at the man on the right, missing his head by four inches; his bullet splashing the dust mud wall. The bullets impact showed Nate where to adjust his sights. In a split second, he manipulated the bolt, held his sights low, and fired once more. This time he found his mark, the bullet tore into the fighter, dropping him to the ground. The fighter's partner had barely enough time to glance at his dying buddy before Nate chambered another round and plugged him, too. Then he shot them both again to make sure they died.

We predicted that the bulk of the enemy's assets would remain oriented to the south. That became apparent, when small groups of fighters started moving towards us using the compounds and tree lines there for cover. Rob and

Team Four tore into the groups. When they didn't have clear shots, we did. When the enemy fighters tried maneuvering on Team Four, they exposed themselves to us. If we weren't able to kill them, we pinned them down and let our JTAC have his fun.

The JTAC (Joint Terminal Attack Controller) was next to me. His job was calling in supporting fire. He was capable of guiding any fixed or rotor wing aircraft in to support us. Early in the fight, we noticed an enemy team carting an AGS-17, a Soviet-designed 30-millimeter automatic grenade launcher. The JTAC guided two close air support aircraft known as A10s, onto them. Smoke and fire engulfed them as they disappeared, and all afternoon the remaining 30mm grenades exploded in the distance.

The fight reached its peak by mid-afternoon, and the next step of our plan unfolded smoothly. Our teams initiated small arms fire, intending to draw the enemy's main effort to maneuver on us. At the same time, India Company moved to the entrance of the valley to the south, essentially clogging the opponents' escape route and creating a kill box.

Like clockwork, the fighters fell into our trap. They skirted the tree line in small groups, trying to close on us. We opened fire killing some and pinning others in irrigation ditches. Other insurgents were trying reinforce by vehicle; they were shot. Those pinned down eventually faced the wrath of British Apaches or US Cobras and A-10s. Before long, piles of smoldering rubble, vehicles, and dead bodies lay scattered everywhere.

Soon we found the man that we'd been looking for, Mr. Khar, one of Northern Helmand province's high-level commanders. By all accounts, he was a tall man, six foot six inches to be exact. Nate, who'd been scouring his suspected compound, sighted a thin, lanky man climbing on a roof. He appeared to be speaking into a handheld radio.

"Tell me exactly what you hear," said Nate to the Marine monitoring enemy radio traffic.

"What's their location?"

"Are the brothers hurt?"

"That's definitely him," replied the other Marine. Mr. Khar was on his roof trying to get a grasp on the situation and had carelessly revealed his position. That sealed his fate.

He was 1,100 meters away, a tough shot with the .50 caliber SASR (Special Applications Scoped Rifle), so we chose the Javelin, a shoulder-fired anti-tank missile. Having been able to pack two of them plus M240 machine guns, sniper rifles, M16s, and grenade launchers were one benefit of larger teams. Creap, a sniper, and prior 0351 infantry assault man was ecstatic at the chance of firing a Javelin. Creap locked the sites of the $80,000 missile on the roof where Mr. Khar unsuspectingly stood. Seconds later, it turned into dirt and debris.

There was no way he survived. We weren't able to confirm his death. However, enemy radio traffic explained it all.

"Did he make it out? Did he make it out?"

"Send the warriors in to get him!"

With that, we unleashed the lions.

Reaper Five's sector had been relatively quiet until the Javelin shot. Then trucks and motorcycles flooded down the wadi from the north towards the fight. Staff Seargent Deptola, our platoon sergeant, and Reaper Five's M240 gunner fired a few bursts to warn the vehicles to stop. Simultaneously, Josh guided three M1A1 Abrams tanks into the wadi from the same direction. A glimpse of the three nearly 70-ton Abrams stopped the other vehicles in their tracks.

We learned earlier in the deployment that snipers and tanks were a perfect match. Our ability to locate and pinpoint targets combined with their 120mm smoothbore main guns made killing Taliban easy. Their main guns could send rounds out past 4,000 meters. In that valley, it was all we needed. But we also used them to defend against reinforcements in the form of enemy vehicles. Taliban cavalry usually amounted to mid-size trucks mounted with heavy weapons, particularly .50 caliber DsHKs (pronounced 'Dishka').

The ground shook under the massive weight of the tanks. That inadvertently scared a lone fighter towards Reaper Five. He rode a motorcycle with an AK and an RPG on his back. There was no telling if he planned to engage the tanks or Josh's team; either way he didn't live long. The machine gunner for Reaper Five mowed him down with a ten round burst. The man fell, but surprisingly climbed back onto his motorcycle and barricaded himself in a small hut nearby. I'm not sure if he bled out from the bullet wounds or not, but I do know that he didn't live through one round from the Abrams tank. It leveled the small building he hid in. When it hit, the concussion caused his motorcycle to explode.

Josh needed to get tanks on the ridge to hold the high ground. He led them into place, but they headed towards a set of pre-dug fighting positions. We knew it was a danger area.

"Tiger one, be advised. Do not maneuver towards the fighting positions," said Josh.

The holes were most likely dug by the Russians decades earlier. The problem was they were magnets for Taliban anti-tank mines and IEDs, and, in fact, Josh's team had found an anti-tank mine near one month's before.

The tanks responded and set in covering 180 degrees to include the wadi and into the valley. The traffic ceased, but Josh spotted a group of men huddled near a car. "Tiger One this is Reaper Five can you glass the white sedan near the green zone?" said Josh. Green zone meant the tree lines and dark vegetated areas.

"Yeah, you talking about the one with a woman and children?" replied the tank commander.

"Negative!" said Josh, and he relayed a better azimuth.

"Got it. We got seven guys, and RPGs."

"Copy. Can you engage?"

Josh already knew the answer was yes.

Another shot from the tank's main gun killed them all. Around the same time, Reaper Four realized that they were on top of an old fighting position. Rob worried that they'd get hit, since we'd already lost two of our brother's months earlier to IEDs. One died; the other lost his leg. Those casualties hit us hard. Fortunately, Reaper Four's area turned out to be clear.

Later, Reaper Five found more targets. They identified three spotters on a roof. It only took one round from the tank to make them disappear as well.
Spotters were always a serious threat. They relayed our movements and called in ambushes or mortars and rockets on us. It happened before, especially to Josh's team. At one point during the deployment, they were shot at every single time they left the wire.

Reaper Two also kept pressure on the enemy. Nate spotted a fighter dashing from the tree line into an alley, moving straight towards us. He was 250 meters away. One shot from Nate and he keeled over. The fighter net to him tried grabbing him and pulling his body to safety, but in order to do so, he was exposed to us. Nate and I both lined up on him and fired. He dropped, too.

While we fought, I couldn't help but notice the civilians. Though I'd seen it over and over before, I was still amazed how accustomed to warfare they were. We were, trading bullets with the Taliban while aircraft rained death from above; Taliban fighters weaved in and out of their village trying to kill us with machine guns and AK's. The entire time, civilians went about their lives, business as usual; baking bread, doing laundry, you name it. It was as if we weren't even there.

After a while, the wind calmed. A friend and fellow sniper once said that when the wind went soft and steady, as it just did, it was a sign from God that the Taliban needed to die that day. I'm not sure if that was true, but I know that those conditions made it a whole lot easier for us to get first-round hits on long-range targets, which, after all, was our specialty.

Shortly afterward, I put his theory to the test. We spotted two insurgents moving through the tree line from the south, towards a compound they had been using all morning. One was older. He had a long flowing white beard and wore a pale blue dishdash or man dress as we called it. A long barreled AK hung from his shoulder. Next to him a younger man in a brown man dress appeared injured. His clothing indicated a scout or low-level fighter. They used the color to blend with the vegetation along the valley floor. It occurred to us that he had been the one pulling the cart for the AGS-17 and had miraculously survived the bombing.

The two made it behind a compound wall but appeared later moving towards another compound. They assumed that they were unseen by using vegetation to hide their movement.

Nate found them. He spotted them moving in and out of the dense vegetation and around the mud walls of the compounds and guided Brendan, his radio operator, and me onto their location.

I focused my scope on them, noticing they were about to get away.

"They're moving towards the red compound door," said Nate. Brendan immediately began to spot for me and checked for wind. The scope on my M40A5 was dialed to 500 meters. The two insurgents were 436 meters away. In seconds, I calculated the equation in my head.

There's a sixty-four meter difference between my DOPE and the target. Hold one mil low and drop it another . 2 for the angle, I thought. Marine snipers learn angle shooting either uphill or downhill at Mountain Sniper Course. The information is extremely valuable in settings like Afghanistan.

"I got the old man," I said, setting my crosshairs ahead of him. I preferred the ambush method when shooting moving targets, meaning I'd shoot in front of the target letting him walk into the bullet.

My lead on the old man set the crosshairs on the younger guy. He looked like death was almost on him. The blood from his wounds had soaked into his clothes. I couldn't imagine he'd live much longer. As far as I was concerned, he and the old man trailing behind him could die together. They had it coming for trying to kill us.

Just before they entered the compound, I squeezed the trigger. The rifle recoiled sending the 175-grain bullet, traveling more than 2,600 feet per second, into the air. It hit the old man near his temple where his beard and cap joined and sent his brains splattering across the door behind him. He died instantly.

"Holy shit that was awesome. It looked just like a movie", whispered Brendan.

Nate was also impressed.

I'll remember that shot for the rest of my life. Not because of the kill, or that I'd displaced a man's brain from his head. For no other reason than that it was the last shot I'd make as a Marine Scout/Sniper in combat. Little did I know, within a few months my world would come crashing down.

Not long after that kill, I let the boys know it was time to go. We had annihilated the area and fucked up the enemy's world. The teams couldn't have executed any better, and now there was no need to stick around. Before we moved, we called in an artillery strike. Instead of explosives, they peppered the valley with a thick, gray smokescreen to mask our exfiltration. As we moved, the heat quickly took a toll on us, and one of the attachments fell victim to heat exhaustion. He could barely stand. We spread his gear and moved on until we made it to the extract site.

Exfil

Back at base, we debriefed the mission and reported the damage. In total, we'd killed thirty-seven. Officially, the US military doesn't keep a record of kills. You can bet that snipers do. Early on we developed a system of integrity by team leaders and assistant team leaders. In order to report the kill, either the Team Leader or Assistant Team Leader had to witness it or visually ID the body. If the body fell out of sight, say in a poppy field or a tree line, it wasn't tallied unless five people completely agreed upon it.

Later, the intelligence officer confirmed what we already believed.

"Good shit, Staff Sergeant Chamblin, your guys killed Mr. Khar."

Even if I wanted to, I couldn't take the credit. The teams deserved the limelight. Of four combat deployments, this was the most successful sniper platoon I'd be a part of, and by the end, the platoon's reputation had spread. Sometime before, General Toolan, the then commanding officer of II Marine Expeditionary Force and Afghanistan's Regional Command Southwest, visited our battalion to meet our platoon and congratulate us for our exploits. Considering his command extended to 20,000 troops, it was a big deal. I was on a mission when he stopped by and wasn't able to meet him.

I did meet the Corps' top brass though, just before we flew back to the States. Apparently the Commandant and Sergeant Major of the Marine Corps were in country and had been briefed on our platoon's success. They specifically requested to have breakfast with just the platoon and me, nobody else. I knew right then that we had done something special.

It was a combination of things. In our current deployment, we'd incorporated additional assets to our teams. Combat engineers, HET (Human Intelligence Exploitation Teams), signals and radio intelligence operators, EOD (Explosive Ordnance Disposal), and JTAC's, but by far, the most devastating was tanks. Rob called our teams mini-CAGs (Combined Arms Group) or Delta Force. I didn't care what we called then; they changed how we deployed as snipers. We reached the point where snipers became the main effort for our battalion operations. We'd come a long way from years prior when we deployed as company support or to watch roads for IEDs.

I wasn't delusional about the accolades; I knew the praise was because we excelled at our job. Plain and simple, we killed a lot of people. That was our fundamental purpose as snipers. The reality is that all snipers in combat turn into competitive killers.

Make no mistake my men weren't bloodthirsty murderers. They were trained snipers determined to hunt bad guys, and they were damn good at it. Among the platoon, every team wanted the most kills. By the end of our stay, the final damage to the enemy was incredible. Reaper One had racked up twenty-six, Reaper Two had fifty-six, Reaper Three had twenty, Reaper Four had eighty-six, and Reaper Five had thirty-five. Those 223 kills came by rifle and small arms fire while tanks and supporting arms killed another 100 or so.

Before we left the country, we met with the Commandant and Sergeant Major of the Marine Corps at Camp Leatherneck. The men were excited to meet the Commandant, but even more so, to meet Sergeant Major Barrett. He was an old sniper and now the senior enlisted man in all the Corps.

The Commandant reserved a section of the chow hall for us. We enjoyed a hearty breakfast. At one point, the Commandant approached me.

"Good job and great leadership," he said with a firm handshake.

I replied with the truth.

"It wasn't me; it was my men."

While I enjoyed the notoriety, a few things ate at me.

We lost one Marine, Sergeant Mark Bradley; six others suffered wounds. I'd had friends killed in combat, but this was different. Never before had I lost anyone in my platoon, let alone under me. By far, having to write a letter explaining his death to his wife, parents, and loved ones was the hardest thing I had to do. It made me sick to my stomach.

A Brewing Storm

We made it home in October 2011, and I immediately volunteered for another deployment to Afghanistan. My wife thought I'd lost it, but I wanted to stay in the fight, knowing that the war was winding down and my operational time as a scout/sniper was getting shorter by the day. I put in my paperwork to 'cross deck' and transfer to First Battalion, Eighth Marines, who were slated to leave within months.

Finally, January 13th rolled around. Six hours before jumping on a flight to Afghanistan, I received a phone call. The Battalion Executive Officer said we needed to talk. I quickly reported to his office.

There was no small talk. "Gunny here is gonna take you to talk to a few gentlemen."

By the look on his face, I knew it was serious. As we walked to the parking lot, Gunny said, "We're going to NCIS (Naval Criminal Investigation Service)." I had expected something like this but hoped it would blow over, so I could get back to sniping.

Once there, we walked down the hallway and into an office with a large door and bulletproof window. Inside, the Sergeant at the desk told me to have a seat, and someone would be out shortly. I immediately had the suspicion that that they were using the same tactics I'd learned in SERE (Survival, Evade, Resistance, Escape) training. Making me sit here was part of their interrogation method. Here though, at least no one would be beating my ass.

After a few hours, I was led into a cold room. The chair I was offered was right under an air conditioning vent. I thought to myself, 'Really guys? You gotta' do better than that.'

They worked hard trying everything to get me out of my comfort zone. They introduced themselves as Naval

Criminal Investigations Officers, federal agents. I don't remember their names. I knew right away what they wanted.

Our conversation was brief. They asked for my basic information, standard military stuff, name, rank, and serial number. They explained the reason for the visit. They were investigating a video released on the Internet. The video showed me and three others urinating on three Taliban fighters. They then read me my rights. I knew that there'd be a backlash, but never thought the issue would go nearly as far as it did.

I replied, "Here's the name of my lawyer. I refuse to waive my rights ... end of interview."

Minutes after walking out of that office, I received official orders from Headquarters Marine Corps. I was now temporarily assigned to Second Marine Regiment until further notice. I would not be going back to Afghanistan with 1/8. It was the start of a shit storm that would reluctantly lead me and my men into infamy.

At first I was sure the Marine Corps would take care of its own. It wasn't long before I realized that wasn't so. My first encounter with Second Marine Regiment was shocking. They served me with a Military Protective Order. It was designed to isolate me and keep me from talking to any of my Marines from 3/2 who I'd just return with from Afghanistan. It was horrifying; the only men I could relate to were the men who'd fought next to me. I was unable to connect with my Marines. Forced to sit on the sidelines as the system and a few asshole senior Marines played political kiss ass, humiliating and destroying the platoon I had built.

Still, I figured at least the whole affair would pass quickly. I wanted it over, so I could link up with 1/8 snipers in Afghanistan. I talked it over with my lawyer, Mr. Gittins, and he drafted the first of many pretrial agreements submitted and denied by the convening authority, General Waldhauser, and after him, General Mills.
Our first proposal was to face the lowest punishment called, Non-Judicial Punishment. They answered, "No." I then asked to be tried in a summary court-martial. Again they replied, "No."

In a matter of days the platoon that once was the Commandant and Sergeant Major of the Marine Corps' poster children, became the bastards that they no longer wanted to be connected with in any way. It became very clear that the political powers and influence would not rest until they made an example of someone. Their first action came with the official delay of promotion letter that I had received the day before. It stated that I would no longer receive my promotion to Gunnery Sergeant. That was February 1, 2012.

All of it was hard for me to digest. I felt angry and betrayed by the Marine Corps and my country. I was most angry at the way the Corps had treated my men. Instead of receiving the credit they deserved, they were bastardized by the system and senior leadership, who could not see past one isolated incident. They refused to recognize all the good these men had accomplished. Their actions in Afghanistan as Marines and scout/snipers should have helped rewrite Marine Corps doctrine on sniping. Instead, their accomplishments went unnoticed, buried in the politics of the day.

The only men who stood by me were those who fought with me, particularly my fellow snipers. It felt as though my life was slipping away right before my eyes. It scared me. Everything I'd done for my country and Corps, everything I planned on doing with my life was now in jeopardy. Being a Marine was something I'd wanted as a boy. It was the very brotherhood to which I'd dedicated my life.

2 INTO THE BROTHERHOOD

Childhood

I joined the Marine Corps at 12 years old. Figuratively
speaking of course, but that's when I made up my mind. I'm
not sure if it's true for every country boy, but in southern
Ohio patriotism is in the blood. My family's fought in every
war this country has had since the Civil War. We even have a
distant relative who fought against the Shawnee with Daniel
Boone in the woods of Kentucky.

As a kid, I listened intently while my great-
grandfathers spoke of the World Wars. I was fascinated. My
grandfather spent two years with the 2nd Infantry Division
in the Korean War, and my uncles fought in Vietnam.
Military service was my destiny.

Like most kids raised in the foothills of the Appalachian Mountains, I loved the outdoors, I spent the majority of my childhood in the woods. Both my mother's and father's families had come from the mountains in the southeastern United States. They were descendants of the Scottish, English, and Irish settlers who fought and intermingled with the Native Americans while helping tame a wild land. It's a beautiful landscape of mature hardwoods that canvas the sweeping countryside and border open hills and endless farms. The fields transform to green with beans and corn in the spring, and the surrounding hills turn rich with color in the fall.

My mother's father settled on a farm in Adams County, Ohio, in 1953. He'd returned from Korea and left the coal mines of Eastern Kentucky for a better life. Later, my mother and father built a house on a corner of his land. He raised cattle and hogs, along with harvesting grain. A successful farmer is a hardworking farmer, and hard work was instilled in me early on.

There, a man's worth is measured by the calluses on his hands. My father had plenty. Growing up, I watched him work multiple jobs while building a residential construction company from scratch. It wasn't unusual for him to work a nightshift at the local power plant and turn right around and apply siding to a house the next day. All you had to do was watch him work, and you'd learn a strong work ethic. I did. My mother also worked, but from home mostly. Later, she drove a school bus.

When I decided to join the Marines, I also decided to shape my life towards that goal. I knew I needed to be smart and strong to succeed in the Corps, so I studied hard and played sports. As soon as I could, I joined cross-country. Then I figured a Marine should know how to fight, so I learned to box. My parents thought it'd be better to do it in an organized sport than at school.

I followed my plan to be a Marine throughout school. I wasn't a star athlete, I tried my best at sports, knowing that at least I would be in good shape, and it would help me to fulfill my goal. In school, I daydreamed of storming far off beaches and fighting to the death against demon foes. My ambitious young spirit couldn't wait to go to war somewhere.

In school, I blended in. I made friends easily enough but always felt that a handful of good friends was worth more than a crowd of acquaintances. In some sense, I was just a shadow on the wall, everyone knew me, but I never tried to stand out much. Academically, I did well and graduated with honors. In sports, I lettered in cross-country and track.

I enjoyed hanging out with my friends when I wasn't working, which seemed to be most of the time. When I could, I took advantage of the outdoor life and spent my time hiking, fishing, hunting, shooting, or camping. When deer season rolled around, our school would shut down for the week. Hunting was that important. I guess they got sick of everyone skipping school then. Eventually though, school came to an end, and I couldn't be more excited. I was off to fulfill my dream of becoming a United States Marine.

First Enlistment

In retrospect, my first enlistment wasn't too exciting. But in August of 1995 I got my wish and shipped off to Recruit Training Depot, Parris Island. I can assure you all of the lore about Marine Corps boot camp is true. It was a complete shock to a small town boy like me.

Immediately upon arrival, we fresh recruits were stripped of any personal identity and were the living, breathing property of the United States Marine Corps. For starters, were taught how to snap and pop with the rifle while marching. To listen the way the Marine Corps wanted us to listen; which was similar to what my father had already taught me.

Every day started before sunup and didn't end until moonrise. There was never a dull moment. The entire experience consisted of learning endless amounts of information about the Marine Corps and physically becoming a Marine. We ran nearly everywhere we went. If not running, we marched and drilled. We also ran obstacle courses and mud runs just for fun.

Parris Island was full of amazing wonders. Alligators, venomous vipers, quicksand, spiders, and the worst of them all, the sand fleas. Those little monsters could eat you alive, yet no one dared swat them. If you did, you'd attract something worse, the Drill Instructors. They were some of the meanest and angriest men I'd ever encounter. One, in particular, Drill Instructor Sergeant Haney, might have been insane. He was as tough as they come, but really cared about his Marines. He was an infantryman first; he made it a point to teach us something worthwhile in combat every day. He and I would meet up years later in Fleet, and work together. He would earn a Silver Star in 2003 for his actions in Operation Iraqi Freedom.

As a young man, a new Marine recruit, I didn't understand what was happening. I did know I wanted the Drill Instructors off my back, so I did as ordered. At the time, I didn't realize that I was learning instant obedience to orders; the exact recipe needed to win in combat. Little by little, they stripped me from my old ways, transforming me into a machine ready to obey.

Later in boot camp, I gladly found my boxing lessons paid off. During the hand-to-hand combat portion of training, I found myself put in a confined square with a fellow Marine named Webster from South Carolina. We strapped on the gloves, and before he knew it, he was out cold. The prize was a phone call home. I was happy to win the prize.

Boot camp sucked. They gave me all the PT, or physical training I could handle. I was happy to becoming a Marine. I looked forward to shooting the M16. The Rifle Range was near the end of our training. We were finally able to fire the weapon. I quickly found I had a knack for hitting my targets. Squirrel hunting with my Dad and Grandpa paid off. I qualified Expert on the Rifle Range.

I learned a lot about the Marine Corps in boot camp, but I learned a more about myself. I learned I could accomplish just about anything. The boot camp experience reconfirmed a childhood lesson, anything worth having was worth working for.

As I look back today, boot camp was my introduction to killing, which is the fundamental purpose of a United States Marine. We learned all about killing and embraced everything to do with it. It encompassed our language and our actions. Hell, "kill" even became the proper response to a given order. Not that I minded. I thoroughly enjoyed the idea.

My time in South Carolina went a lot faster than I anticipated, and before long, it was Graduation day. All my family came down to see me. It was three long months of boot camp and several years of waiting to get here. I was proud my family was here to watch me accomplish a goal I'd had for so long. My new life brought a sense of adventure and fun. I couldn't wait to get on with my Marine life. I went home for the obligatory ten days of leave, then reported to the School of Infantry, in Camp Geiger, North Carolina. Marine Combat Training.

Before my joining the Marines, my Uncle, who was two years my elder, served as an infantryman. He convinced me to sign up as a mechanic so I'd have a future outside of the Corps. I obliged. After my infantry training, I'd head to mechanics school. I spent a month and a half at Camp Geiger training for the infantry. It turned out to be six weeks of shooting, hiking, running, hiking, classes on weapons, hiking, running, hiking, digging fighting holes, hiking, hand-to-hand combat and more hiking. Did I mention we did a lot of running and hiking?

I left Camp Geiger high on life and ready to take on the world. With a quick trip up the New River, I arrived at Camp Johnson, Montford Point, North Carolina. I was there for a year of basic and advanced training as a diesel mechanic. I learned more than I ever wanted to know about military vehicles and diesel engines. I quickly discovered the life of a Marine wasn't exactly what I thought it would be. At least not as a POG, Personnel Other than Grunt. It turned out to be just like any other job, with the exception of no overtime pay. And we worked a lot of overtime, with no pay.

While at Camp Johnson, I met my first wife, Becky. It was love, at first sight. We were both young, I fell head over heels for her, and married quickly followed. About the same time, I received orders to Camp Lejeune, North Carolina. I joined 2nd Maintenance Battalion, 2nd Force Service Support Group. It was just another short trip up the New River.

I hated being a mechanic, but it paid the bills and brought me home most nights. I worked there for the next three years, during which time my first wife and I had my daughter, Whitney. I didn't know I could love someone as much as I loved that little bundle of snot and dirty diapers.

Before I knew it, I was getting my first divorce. Becky left my daughter with me and split. That was a tough time. I was a single father trying to raise a daughter. I decided to get out of the Marines and raise my little girl back home in Ohio.

When I returned to Ohio, I went back to working residential and commercial construction with my father. Financially and personally I was doing well, but I missed the camaraderie of the Marines. I decided that the reserves would be a good fit for me as a single parent. I also had no desire to be a mechanic, so I joined a combat engineer unit in Charleston, West Virginia. Alpha Company, 4th Combat Engineer Battalion, 4th Marine Division.

I eagerly learned how to be a combat engineer. Essentially, we shot weapons and set off explosives every weekend. Life didn't get a whole lot better than that. We trained throughout West Virginia, Kentucky, Virginia, and North Carolina. The unit sent me to the Basic and NCO Reserve Combat Engineer Schools at Court House Bay, North Carolina. Then to the Urban Mobility Breacher Course in Quantico, Virginia.

Things were looking up. I was back in the Marines and even had a combat MOS this time around. I had a decent job in Ohio working for my father's construction company, I had my Marines, so I was fairly content with life for the time being.

My personal life was looking up as well. I had met a beautiful young lady named Kayla at a local church. Kayla and I began dating in February of 2001. She loved my daughter and me, and we all seemed to fit together perfectly.

Cornerstone

In April of 2001, I was still part of a platoon from Alpha Company, 4th Combat Engineer Battalion (CEB), 4th Marine Division. We deployed to Albania with a company of infantrymen from Alabama. We were part of Operation Cornerstone.

Though I'd already served four years on active duty, this was my first trip overseas. Our detachment was part of a security and force preservation mission that lasted about a month. It wasn't long enough to count as a sea service deployment in the Corps, but it proved to be a good experience nonetheless.

Our primary mission was to provide security for the Navy's famed Seabees. They rebuilt damaged roads and bridges and improved the NATO and Albanian military positions in the area. My job was the SOG or Sergeant of the Guard along with a 3/23 infantry Marine from Alabama named Hollis. He told me I should've been a grunt. Maybe he had a premonition. Hollis was a good Marine and good person who worked hard and looked out for his men. The grunt's from Alabama were a joy to work. We were both excited to be doing something other than our normal drill for the year.

When we weren't providing security for the Seabees and repairing bunkers on the base, we conducted cross-training with demolitions and weapons alongside the Albanian and Macedonian Commandos. They were especially impressed with the improvised explosives we taught them. Looking back, I'm still not 100 percent sure teaching them this was a good idea. I often wonder why they were so interested in improvised explosives? Nonetheless, the training went well, and it was a good experience for all of us

Being there was an eye opener. It was the first time I'd see anything like it. The people lived in desperate conditions following the Baltic war and the genocide during the mid and late '90s. The war-torn country was bombed out with burned buildings everywhere you looked. The countryside, however, was scenic and beautiful and reminded me of Charleston, West Virginia, and the mountains that my Marine unit called home.

The amount of poverty was sad. The people there desperately tried to rebuild their nation after years of war. Ironically enough, we were there to help the ethnic Albanians, the majority of which are Muslim, to rebuild their country. I would not fully appreciate this irony until later in life, after the attack on the United States on September 11, 2001. Regardless, at the time it was nice to help people that were having such a hard go of things.

It came as a surprise that organized crime there regulated the locals and controlled the markets in the area.

They were primarily from the Italian, Greek, and Russian organizations and were easy to spot. Their imported American cars and tailored suits were in stark contrast to the shabby clothes of the merchants and farmers who worked the local markets. Other than the occasional run-in with one of these thugs, there wasn't much of a direct threat to the Seabees or us. The only interaction with the mobsters was when one of our posts reported seeing a man get shot and thrown over a bridge into a river after an apparent hit.

Nightly, red and green tracers from heavy machine guns flew back and forth in the neighboring Kosovo. Mortars and artillery shell explosions roared in the distance. That sparked my curiosity about real combat, and I wondered what it would be like. The entire month there, we got shot at once, but it turned out to be a whole lot of posturing and a couple of rounds flying overhead.

During this short time in the war-torn Baltic region, I realized just how much I missed the camaraderie of the Corps. There is nothing like a trip to a third world dump to put life into perspective and make men bond. It lasted only a few weeks, and though I considered reenlisting, it wasn't until later that year that my decision to do so would be locked in. When the terrorist attacks happened in New York City, Pennsylvania, and the Pentagon on September 11, 2001, I knew what I had to do.

3 JOINING THE FIGHT

9/11

I was working in a house way back in the hills of Ohio on that cold, fall morning of September 11, 2001. We were remodeling a kitchen when the News Flash came over the TV. Everyone instantly stopped working after realizing the seriousness of the situation. We were utterly captivated. When the second plane hit, I immediately packed my tools, jumped in my truck, and raced home. The first call I made was to my Platoon Commander, asking him if we were gearing up. I expected that we'd activate and ship off to war, but that didn't happen.

The reality was no one knew what was going to happen. Initially, we didn't even know who instituted the attacks or why. As the information pointed to Al Qaeda and radical Islam, I knew that our country would find those responsible, and I wanted to be there when that happened. I wanted to fight just as the generations before me had. The young man in me didn't even blink at the thought of going to combat. It was something that I needed to do.

The next few months were a blur. When I finally realized my reserve unit wasn't going to war, I made the decision to drop everything and serve again. I wouldn't be able to live with myself if this country was at war and I didn't join in. I knew I needed to talk to a prior service recruiter. I found him and marched into his office.

"I want back in."

"Ok. You wanna' go back to being a mechanic or engineer?"

"No. I wanna' be 03, infantry."

The recruiter explained that he had slots for 0331, machine gunners.

"Sign me up," I replied.

By the time I cut through the paperwork bullshit, it was February of 2003, eighteen months since 9/11. My new unit, 2nd Battalion, 8th Marines, was already on the northern border of Saudi Arabia preparing to invade Iraq. I was stuck assisting recruiters in my hometown. I drove a government vehicle around picking up 'poolees', future recruits. I picked them up and dropped them off and was tired of listening to those future boots bitch and moan all the time. I wanted to be in Iraq mixing it up with the bad guys.

Infantry

My misery came to an end in August of 2003. I reported back to Camp Lejeune and checked into 2d Battalion, 8th Marine Regiment, 2nd Marine Division. The men returning after having participated in the invasion of Iraq were pumped full of excited energy. That mood changed, and everyone seemed disappointed when we got the news we were redeploying to Afghanistan. We'd be leaving in November of 2003. Our Battalion would have only four short months to prepare.

I'd now be part of Weapons Company, and the Combined Anti-Armor Team or CAAT (pronounced 'cat') Platoon. Heavy machine guns, TOW gunners, assault men, and dismounted infantry made up the unit. I knew it would be completely different from being a mechanic or engineer.

When I checked into the company office, I ran into a familiar face.

"I know you!" said Gunnery Sergeant Haney.

"You were my drill instructor," I replied.

He walked away smiling. I remembered him; he cared about his Marines, and that was a comforting thought, knowing he'd be there with us in combat.

In order for our unit to deploy at manning level, we received about 300 men from 1st Battalion, 2d Marines. That's when I met Ben and Williams, two of the many Marines from 1/2. We eventually became good friends, and I looked to them for advice, along with Kreuger and the others from CAAT Alpha and Bravo.

When I arrived at my platoon, some Marines were a little apprehensive about me. Rightfully so, since I'd never served in the infantry, yet as a Sergeant, I outranked almost everyone. To me that didn't matter, I was determined to prove that I belonged.

The job of a CAAT team was to conduct mounted operations in support of the battalion, more specifically, to target armored assets and reinforced positions. We didn't anticipate enemy armor in Afghanistan, so we trained for vehicle patrols and did gun drills over and over. We took the various weapon systems and practiced assembling them as fast as possible, then train them on various types of targets and ranges. It takes a very coordinated effort on the part of the machine gun team, each member of the team each needs to perform flawlessly and independently, without instruction. I did these drills alongside the boots. A Sergeant running gun drills alongside Lance Corporals wasn't good for my image, but I truly had no shame. I needed to learn just as everyone else, and in the end, it helped earn me the respect of my Marines.

Everything I learned about the machine gun was through OJT (On the Job Training). I tried to learn as much as I could about my new job in the infantry from the Marines around me. I also read all the information I could get my hands on, from weapons manuals and military doctrinal publications, to stories from machine gunners and infantrymen in Vietnam.

I learned to employ machine guns in the most effective manner. It required knowing the various forms of fires, such as enfilade, plunging, and the basics of fire employment. Marine Corps use, in general, in particular, the principles of employment explained by the acronym PICMDEEP. The acronym stood for Pairs, Interlocking (fields of fire), Coordination (of fire), Mutual (support), Defilade, Enfilade, Entrenchment, and Protection. Before long, I knew everything about machine guns and how to effectively deploy them.

During this time, I read a book about Marine Scout/Snipers in Vietnam. I made the decision that day to do whatever necessary to become a scout/sniper. Among other things, I wanted to be the one hunting down the enemy, not the one being hunted.

When I demonstrated that I knew everything about the weapon, the Battalion Gunner signed off on my training. I was now a full-fledged 0331. I felt great learn the trade. It felt even better having the confidence in my abilities, knowing that I now 'belonged' in the infantry. I couldn't wait to test my skills in combat.

As the days to departure shortened, the work got harder. We trained in the field every week. I got to know the men I would deploy with; men like Ben, a no-nonsense Marine from New Jersey. He'd join us from First Battalion, Second Marines. Then there was old man Bolland, a comical fellow from Georgia. I got especially close got to the guys in my truck. Doc Vause was our section's Corpsman, from Jacksonville, Florida. There was John Cain a Grunt from Oklahoma, our Gunner, Moks, from Seattle. Good guys who taught me my first lesson as a leader of infantrymen. It was the exact thing my father used to tell me: Never ask a man to do anything you are not willing to do yourself or do with him.

The other lessons showed up in the little things we did every day. Suffering in the field with your Marines when you didn't have to be there was big. Never screaming at men you out ranked to make yourself look good was mandatory for respect. I learned to base my decisions as a leader on how those decisions would benefit those below me. My leadership lessons quickly earned the respect of the men around me. That's a lesson many at the Staff Non-Commissioned Officer (SNCO) and above in the Marine Corps should learn. Instead of making decisions that only benefit one's career, leaders should make decisions that benefit the men they're leading into combat.

As we prepared to deploy my family prepared for our separation. My family was growing. I had a new wife who readily adopted my daughter, and we had a new baby, a son. Life was good, with the exception of my coming deployment. The Corps was hard on families. Marines, especially the infantry, were always gone. We were either deployed or in the field training. When we weren't in the field, we were attending a military school somewhere.

That's rough on spouses. Needless to say, my wife was apprehensive about me leaving as any wife would be. I assured her that I'd be out of harm's way.

A-STAN

November, 2003 came as we set off for the high mountains of Afghanistan and the Hindu Kush. I said goodbye to Kayla and the kids and boarded the plane. Leaving my family for this long and knowingly going into a combat zone was hard. Part of me, well a lot of me was going to miss them. They were my life, but I also had a duty as an American and a Marine, fighting was something I had to do.

I was now a vehicle commander in a heavy machine gun truck. After all the years of training and preparing for combat, I finally felt like a real Marine. I was on my way to Afghanistan with America's Battalion to bring justice to our country's enemies.

We flew into Afghanistan via Turkey and Kyrgyzstan. In Turkey, we stopped for fuel and a short layover. Surprisingly, armed guards patrolled the area and didn't permit us to leave our little sector. I assumed it was for our safety since it appeared the entire Muslim world wanted a crack at the United States. One thing I enjoyed there was the weather was nice enough for a nap on the tarmac.

Kyrgyzstan was different. We landed at a small airbase with a tiny hanger. It was freezing when we got off the plane; with everything covered in snow. Shortly after landing, a blizzard hit, stranding us there. I'd have to say it was one of the coldest places I've ever been. We were given an abandoned hanger to sleep in, with no beds and no heat. Come to find out, the Air Force had established the base a few years earlier and kept the hangers for Marines. They were about a quarter mile away from the main base. A sign at the store summed up their impression of us: "We refuse to serve alcohol to US MARINES!"

My guess is they were tired of us breaking shit. Or maybe it was for doing what Marines do best, getting drunk and fighting. We learned later Marines from another battalion had done just that, cleaned some Airmen's clocks.

After a weeklong stay and a foot of new snow, we finally boarded C-130s and flew to southern Afghanistan. We landed at Bagram Air Field, just north of the Afghan capital of Kabul. Once the planes touched down, we unloaded all of our gear and equipment and moved into our little-quarantined corner of heaven on the air base. It became abundantly clear that the Air Force didn't want us intermingling with their personnel.

I have to admit, I was a little nervous about my first trip into the fray. A man can gather only so much knowledge and perspective about war from friends and books. At the same time though, my confidence in our platoon soared. I knew we all worked well as a team and that my platoon had an excellent base of knowledge. They also had experience from the Marines who'd just come back from the invasion of Iraq.

We set up our operations center on base; then our command became concerned about the security there, and for good reason. The 'locals' working on the base, had the luxury to wander anywhere. The Air Force didn't do a very good job of keeping track of them. We had them to worry about, and we caught other branches of service attempting to help themselves to parts in our motor pool.

Our base camp barely established and we received follow-on orders. The primary objective for Coalition forces at the time was COIN (Counter-Insurgency) operations and nation building. Our battalion was to assist by helping Special Operations Forces. My CAAT section, along with Echo Company were to move north to the Kunar Province along the Pesch and Korengal valleys. We were relieving the Army's 7th Cavalry, who provided security and support to Army Special Forces, Operational Detachment Alpha (ODA) Teams in the areas around Asadabad.

My CAAT team consisted of four armored HMMWVs with about three or four Marines in each vehicle or vic. Doc, Moks, and I would take the lead vic, followed by Bolland, Halle, and Milquette in the second. Des, Bingham, and Hadin had the third vic, and Jeb, Jimmy, and Mr. Fast, along with Weatherford, would bring up the rear.

We staged our gear on the flight line and boarded the Army's Blackhawk helicopters for the ride up north. The birds carried us through the mountain passes to the LZ

(Landing Zone) at Combat Outpost (COP) Asadabad. We arrived at the COP to the welcoming arms of the soldiers from the Seventh Cavalry. They were more than happy to see us, especially since our arrival meant their departure.

The 'locals' weren't so happy to see us. Our first night we took rocket and mortar fire from the surrounding mountains. Lucky for us, the insurgent firing the mortars was stupid. One 82mm mortar landed directly on one of the soldier's cots. Fortunately, he was out taking a piss. The rag head forgot to remove the safety pin, and the mortar was a dud.

We soon realized we were in a cat and mouse game. An indication of what was to come for most of my fighting in Afghanistan. We'd take fire, fire back only to watch the enemy melt into the mountains, or worse, melt into the local population. I'd have to wait to become a sniper for that to change. Looking back, the enemy seemed to be watching and waiting. They weren't as aggressive as later in the war, when I would return for the second time. On this tour, they would take pot shots at us and drop mortars and rockets.

The RIP or Relief in Place was relatively uneventful. The highlight was two Air Force A10s screamed through the valley, popping flares just to show off. A few of Marines from 1/2 were freaked out. It was an A10 that mistakenly killed their comrades during the invasion of Iraq months earlier.

With the Calvary gone, we assumed control over the area. CAAT Bravo along with Echo Company 2/8 took over the Combat Outpost, Observation Points, and Patrol Bases. We also started security patrols throughout Kunar Province.

The mountains were very rugged and sparsely vegetated. What few trees that did grow, grew at high elevation and were small coniferous trees and shrubs. The landscape reminded me a lot of the southwestern United States with its high deserts, but this was a whole new kind of desolation. There were few wild animals. The majority of the animals we saw were the livestock tended by old men and young boys.

From the beginning, it was apparent we were playing catch-up, compared to the 'locals' knowledge of the land and its uses. The enemy had the terrain and local knowledge to their advantage, and it gave them freedom of movement; that, along with their experience with the Russians, gave them a distinct advantage. What they didn't have was our technology and logistical capabilities.

Our small bases were susceptible to indirect attacks. The steep mountains surrounding us allowed small insurgent teams to sneak up and launch rockets and mortars at us. Though I hated to believe it, the insurgents weren't all stupid. Some were rather ingenious in their resourcefulness, especially with the weapons at their disposal. Once they realized we were able to move air assets and respond with mortars on their firing positions, they switched tactics. Some started using kitchen timers for their 107mm and 84mm recoilless rifles. It allowed them to fire the weapons without the risk of counter-battery or an air retaliation. They also used small pieces of ice and wedged them between the 82mm mortars and the firing tube. When the ice melted, the mortar fell and fired with the operator safely out of the area.

The Green Berets we worked with were exceptionally good soldiers and lived up to their hard earned reputation as professionals. They provided a wealth of knowledge when it came to the area, enemy, and terrain, as well as weapons and communications systems.

We patrolled the dusty roads in and out of the Asadabad area. Our area included the Pesch and Korengal valleys and the remote patrol bases to the north and east. We were kilometers from the Pakistan border, and we occasionally took trips up to the edge just to see into the other country.

Since we were mobile with four trucks, we were constantly on the go. We ran recce (reconnaissance) patrols to the outlying areas for ODA (Operational Detachment Alpha) or Army Special Forces. We ran it weapons cache sweeps, vehicle checkpoints (VCPs), and tactical checkpoints (TCPs) along the routes in and out of Pakistan.

During these checkpoints, we would search for contraband weapons, demolitions, or anything they could make into a bomb. We also looked for unusual amounts of currency, multiple identifications as well as people on our list of HVTs (High-Value Targets). During one of the VCPs along the border, we snagged a Pakistani carrying multiple passports and $12,000 in US currency. We turned him over to

ODA, and they flipped him, using the information he had for our operations.

Running ODA operations was my first lesson in counter-insurgency, and the pros in ODA were the ones teaching the lessons. At first, I was extremely aggravated that the bad guy being interviewed by ODA wasn't going to rot in a prison somewhere. But the amount of intelligence garnished from the old man far outweighed the need to lock him up. I learned, that when fighting insurgents, you have to be willing to use your resources to their full potential, even if it means stepping into the gray area. The whole experience turned out to be a very useful learning tool for future operations.

Up north with Echo Company, we helped expand the ODA's area of responsibility (AO). We did it by assisting them in building new patrol bases to the north, near Catamount and Nangalam. We helped by moving supplies to them from Asadabad and providing security along the routes to and from the isolated bases.

One of the patrol bases was Camp Blessing. We had a few small skirmishes near the outpost, but we usually repelled them quickly with air support. The AC130 Specter Gun Ship wiped the Taliban from the mountainside in minutes. It was awesome watching the JTAC call in pass after pass on the fleeing enemy. Insurgents learned quickly, that to survive; they needed to hit and run or face our air power.

There, I got my first up-close and personal brush with IEDs (improvised explosive devices.) They'd just started to catch on in the country. At the time, they used remote controls to detonate the IEDs, but they adapted once we started using equipment to jam their signals. Then they switched to command wire, which they pulled to detonate the bombs. It took our jammers out of the fight.

That first experience with IEDs happened when we went to register target points for the 81mm and 120mm mortars outside COP Asadabad. The idea was to designate known points for the mortars, essentially denying the enemy that terrain, but giving us reference points in case we needed mortars for support in that area.

To do the job properly, we climbed, in trucks, to the top of a ridge line east of the COP. The only road leading there had never seen pavement; in fact, potholes, boulders, and bumps made it difficult to traverse. If that weren't bad enough, it was sandwiched between a cliff and a canal, nullifying any possibility of an alternate route. Plain and simple, it was the ideal place for an IED.

Registering the mortars didn't take long, and we moved down, back towards the base. Since I was the patrol leader, my truck led the way. We crept along the road until reaching a narrow pass just wide enough for one vehicle. The bumps were so bad that they rattled my gunner, Moks, from his turret, and he sat down on the gunner strap as we went over that rough terrain. Good thing he did, because right then a large explosion rocked our truck, filling the cab with a dust filled haze.

An IED detonated under the driver's front tire. The blast was like nothing I'd ever felt. The sheer force shook my bones and rippled through my whole body. As I sat dazed, with my head ringing like a bell, I quickly realized that I was still in one piece, uninjured. I turned to my driver, Doc V and saw he'd been knocked senseless. Poor ol' Moks was scared shitless. I'm pretty sure he was unconscious. I had to punch him in the ass to make sure he was ok, plus I needed him back on the machine gun in case rounds started cracking our way.

It took a second to gather our senses. When we finally did, we rolled forward into a security posture and called for EOD (Explosive Ordnance Disposal) support from the COP. Someone noticed a couple of men running into a compound to the north. Kreuger stopped the remaining trucks, and dismounts began systematically clearing the area while I sent reports up to headquarters. Our Marines captured a handful of assholes, who we later found were responsible for the IED we hit. After loading the assholes up, we rolled back to the COP. My truck limped back, pulled by another truck since the front end was all fucked up.

In the end, we were very lucky. EOD examined the site and found two more 82mm mortars connected, but unfired. They'd misfired, only detonating one. Had they all gone off, we'd have been hamburger meat. Doc was the most fortunate. The blast blanket in his seat had saved him since our HMMVs had no armor. After that, I took my front SAPI plate (Small Arms Protective Insert body armor) and sat on it while in the truck. I didn't care what happened; if we got hit again, I was going home with my balls.

Before this deployment, I never thought about Afghanistan or its people. Being there was like witnessing something from an ancient storybook. As much as I tried, I couldn't understand or respect their primitive culture and archaic logic. They had no concept of life outside of their village or valley. They didn't even believe that man had been to the moon or that the world was round, nor did they care to learn about it. I had learned this from talking to one of the ODAs interpreters. I was amazed.

As intriguing as it was, there was a grim and repulsive side. Their distorted religiosity disgusted me, especially in their treatment of women and children. To the Afghan men, women and children were nothing more than property. The old men beat children with sticks when they didn't listen, and they heard women like cattle. There were even intel reports of women being stoned to death for dishonoring their families and clans in various ways. Civilians were no better than enemy fighters, who prided themselves on being great warriors, but used women and children as shields during firefights. Fucking cowards.

As far as I could tell, the only thing the Afghan people had going for them was their beautiful, mineral-rich landscape. At times, in the Hindu Kush Mountains, I'd stare in awe at mesmerizing sunrises and sunsets. They were truly a sight to see.

After two months in the Hindu Kush, we rotated out and headed back to Bagram Air Field. Our new mission at Bagram was providing Quick Reaction Force (QRF) for the base and our sister units up north. We also did route security to the immediate areas near the air base. Truth be told, it was a slow assignment, but it gave us a well-deserved break. Deep down, there wasn't a Marine in our section who didn't enjoy it.

Life was good. We had plywood shacks with real walls to live in, and an Air Force chow tent on the other end of the base. There was even a shower tent we used a couple times a week to keep the stench off. The only real down-side was the night patrols in the dead of winter. We froze our tails off in the unheated and unarmored trucks. We also managed to hit another IED outside of the base. Thankfully, the explosives weren't large enough to do real damage, plus no truck was in the line of fire. Had we been hit, I trusted the plate under my ass to do its job.

My biggest event was being promoted to section leader. The previous leader had struggled choosing negotiable routes and had a bad habit of totaling trucks. I was put in charge after he destroyed his third vehicle in two rollovers. In his defense, we had no solid intel about the areas where we conducted recce patrols. We used Russian maps for the first few months. At any rate, I was now in charge of the section. Soon after that, we were tasked as the lead element in one of the battalion's largest operations.

The Battalion headed east of Kabul, near the village of Sarobi. Anyone familiar with the Russian war in Afghanistan will remember, this was a highly contested area, due to the hydroelectricity provided by the dam there. We expected the same resistance as we moved in. My section's first mission was to identify and recon the primary and alternate routes in and out of the area. We scouted the main route from Kabul and the alternate route through the mountains coming in from the north. It took nearly a week and was surprisingly uneventful, except the Taliban capturing some foreign aid workers in the Mountains to our south. I'm not sure what became of them, but we continued our mission with more caution.

Our section swept the harsh mountain roads for a week before successfully reporting primary and secondary routes to the Commanding Officer. We also explored sites for the base camp at the dam and patrol bases near the village. It was nice being out on our own, conducting recon for the battalion. By this point, we'd learned how to operate independently. The fact that the Colonel trusted our section was a good feeling and gave us a sense of accomplishment. The living situation during this period sucked. There are only so many ways you can sleep in a truck, none of them comfortable. After the recon, we traveled back to Bagram to prepare for a supposed one-week operation in and around Surobi and its dam.

Surobi was somewhat like an oasis in a desert. It was the region's source of water and electricity. The dam supplied power for the entire area and the majority of Kabul as well. The river supplied the locals with water for their crops and animals. The town itself was the same as every other run-down marketplace full of vendors along the street in open stalls selling their wares.

At Surobi, my section conjoined with a squad from Fox Company. Our element established roving patrol bases and traveled around the dam and village setting up checkpoints along the main road. After seven days, we expected to move back to the main base. That didn't happen. Instead, the mission was extended. I didn't mind the work, but the problem was we'd packed for one week, bringing enough food, water, ammo, and clothing for one week, plus, maybe a few days. The mission eventually lasted forty-seven days.

I can't remember how long we were running missions, but it was so long we had to ration water and chow. By then, everyone was starved from eating only one MRE (Meal Ready to Eat) a day. "Fuck it." I sent a couple of Marines on a patrol to the local market for some food. I imagined a little Afghan BBQ wouldn't hurt anybody.

With two American dollars, they brought back a mound of foot bread, two chickens, and a duck. Where the duck came from we didn't want to know. I hadn't seen one the entire time. To start the cookout, we selected Jason, who'd never killed an animal in his life, to chop up the duck.

That was a mistake. It took him forever to take that duck's head off with an ax. I felt sorry for the animal. Another Marine had been a sous chef before joining the Corps; he concocted a mixture of MRE ingredients and local spices to make a marinade for the duck and chicken meat.

Apparently something serious went wrong with the cooking process, I ended up all night with the shits. In fact, I went all over the one set of clothing I brought with me. I'd only packed for a one-week mission. Consequently, I spent the next twenty-four hours going twenty-six times, totally annihilating all my clothing. Dysentery at its finest.

The next morning, I went to base camp for meds and to wash my clothes. I wore flip-flops, underwear, a flak jacket, and a helmet. Who did I run into? The Battalion Commander and Sergeant Major.

"What the fuck is wrong with you, Marine?" All I could tell the brass was I'd shit all over my clothes. After a laugh at my expense, I went to the river to wash my cammies on a rock. The river wasn't only slightly cleaner than my clothes, but the bath sure felt amazing.

While in the Surobi area, we conducted security operations for Afghan and Coalition Forces meetings and MedCAPs (Medical Civil Action Program, essentially medical assistance for the locals). During the MedCAPs, we provided security while the corpsmen tried helping the locals any way they could. Being onsite allowed us to interact with the locals and show them we weren't part of the problem but part of the solution. It also allowed us the opportunity to collect information about the local Taliban and insurgent activity through the local population's views.

One memorable MedCAP took us to a remote village about thirty kilometers from any other town. It was deep in a valley with only one way in and out that ran through a narrow gorge. The gorge was impassable when it rained. It was one of the most isolated places I'd ever see. I couldn't believe people lived in such primitive way, yet seemed very content. They still lived in stone and mud huts with no electricity or running water. There were no schools or even makeshift stores.

On another patrol, we conducted a route recon into a valley to a small village where we intended to provide a MedCAP. On the way, we came across an area full of poppies. The pink and white flowers in full bloom made for a beautiful backdrop against the lush green valley. There was also a quaint cemetery full of flags and stones. The flags were green, red, black, and white suggesting a strong Taliban presence in the area.

The Taliban were up and down the stream and river valleys. We found the population lived in constant fear, under constant observation from them. On this particular patrol, we were told by one old man that we should leave because there were over 100 Taliban fighters coming to seal off the valley entrance and attack us. The attack never happened, but the fear the locals felt was palpable.

The difference between Western and Afghan cultures is hard to explain. One difference is the value that we place on human life. Once during a VCP at Surobi, a Marine rifleman from Fox Company shot and killed a man who tried to grab his M4. We figured the man must have been crazy, and it turned out he was. Surprisingly enough, his family, who knew of his mental instability, wasn't the least bit upset with his being killed by us. The family thanked us for relieving them of their burden. The mentality blew me away.

For my section, one of the most memorable missions came when we, along with snipers, supported a company raid deep in the mountains east of Surobi. We patrolled the area early in the morning while it was still dark. Snipers already had eyes on the target for twenty-four hours, and we cordoned off the town as the platoon from Fox Company swept the area. We recovered hundreds of weapons and massive amounts of mortars, rockets, and artillery rounds. On extract, one of the HMMWV's became disabled on the road. We couldn't take the truck or equipment out safely, so my section posted security around it. A few scout/sniper teams held over-watch.

Later that night, Milky, one of my machine gunners, spotted an RPG team approaching from the northeast. Our comm equipment was on the fritz, so he left his truck and ran down to my vehicle. Milky was a big dude, about 6'4" and close to 300 pounds. I couldn't help but laugh after his short run. He stood hunched over trying to explain the situation while he sucked wind.

When he finally spit it out, I sent him and a couple of riflemen to the edge of the ridge line with night optics and rifles to check it out. They spotted the RPG team and opened fire with M4s and an M249 SAW wounding one insurgent. The men ran back towards their village once Milky and the boys opened up. I relayed everything to the Battalion COC (Combat Operations Center) and talked a section of Army Apaches onto the RPG team and village. The pilot couldn't distinguish the insurgents from villagers and flew low and slow overhead as a show of force, and then flew back to

Bagram.

In May of 2004, the end of our deployment drew near. We turned the area over to Third Battalion, Sixth Marines and pulled out of the mountains, heading back to Bagram Air Field. Once the entire battalion was back at Bagram, we moved from the north end of the base to a tent city next to the airstrip. We stayed there until our flight back to the world showed up.

While living in 'tent city' I spent a lot of time talking with the guys in the scout/sniper platoon. I talked with Nate, John, and Courtney about weapons and tactics. I was impressed by their appearance, attitude, and professionalism. I'd ask to take the Indoc, a two-week test to get into the sniper platoon, when I first arrived. I was told to learn to become a machine gunner first. I learned they'd be conducting another Selection/Indoctrination when the Battalion returned stateside. I made up my mind I was going to try out.

The evening before leaving 'tent city', we were shelled with 107mm rockets. Fortunately, no one was seriously hurt. Before boarding the C-130 for Kyrgyzstan, I took some sleeping pills to get a rest on the trip. Imagine my surprise when I woke up six hours later, and we were still in Bagram.

Turns out that the bird was having trouble. Oh well, it wouldn't be the Marine Corps without some bullshit. Eventually, we departed, and on the flight, I contemplated my time in Afghanistan. The biggest thing I'd learned was to study the enemy. I'd learned their culture, tactics, patterns, and how they operate. Knowing your enemy is fundamental to win in combat. My first deployment helped me to learn that.

4 HUNTER OF GUNMEN

In Vietnam, the Viet Cong feared few enemy fighters. Their ability to blend with the local population and creep through jungles undisturbed gave them an edge. So too did the insurgents move in and out of Iraq's cities and the villages and mountains of Afghanistan. As bold as they both were, they equally feared US snipers, enough to put bounties on their heads. In particular they feared US Marine Scout Snipers.

In 2004, as Marines in Iraq tore through the insurgent-infested Fallujah, their first assault ended in a cease-fire. The indomitable General "Mad Dog" Mattis met with insurgent leaders. The insurgents first request was simple; call off your snipers. Marine snipers like Ethan Place of Second Battalion First Marines had stacked bodies in the streets and struck fear into insurgents by showing that death could touch them at any moment. For me, as a Marine, I wanted to do the same. Being a sniper would allow me to hunt down the enemies of my country.

In the infantry, there's one Scout Sniper Platoon within each battalion. At one time, it was called STA (Surveillance and Target Acquisition), but anymore it's just SSP (Scout Sniper Platoon). The entrance into that platoon starts with Indoctrination (Indoc), a short but grueling test of mind and body.

We arrived stateside, then, after post-deployment leave, my battalion SSP held their Indoc. I knew it was going to be tough, real tough. It was short, three days total, but we all knew it would be brutal none-the-less.

During the Indoc, we learned the pecking order of a sniper platoon. The Marines running the show were HOGs (Hunters of Gunmen). They'd already graduated from Division sniper school and were the top of the food chain when it comes to Marine snipers. The next step down were the PIGs (Professionally Instructed Gunmen). They were new guys in the platoon, Marines who hadn't made it through school yet. During the Indoc, we were known as lowly SLUGs (Slow Lazy Untrained Gunmen).

Somewhere near the end of my three days, my body nearly gave out on me. With no sleep, little food, and physical thrashings, I was worn out. We all were. During a 15-mile ruck run, I ended up on the side of the road with a few HOGs standing over me.

"Are you ready to quit?" one shouted.

"Nope," I mustered.

"Ok, strip him down."

I removed all my clothes except my underwear. They covered me in ice while a Corpsman inserted an IV into my veins. I'd succumb to dehydration, and heat exhaustion, but that didn't mean I was going to quit. Within minutes, I strapped my ruck on, got up and kept running. I made up my mind I'd never give up. Life in the sniper platoon would be much better than in the regular infantry, and I would've rather died on the side of the road than admit defeat.

The final phase was an interview in front of all the HOGs. We SLUGs were dressed in our Charlie uniforms and grilled by the snipers. It was a test of bearing and confidence. After the interview, they made their selection. I made it! I was part of the six selected to join the platoon. At twenty-six years old I was a fresh PIG. I'd be but under SIP (Sniper Indoctrination Probation), being screened to go to Scout Sniper School.

SSP (Scout Sniper Platoon)

You need a thick skin to be in the Scout Sniper Platoon. The men in the platoon are all Type "A" individuals. They want to be the best at whatever they do. I learned quickly that it paid to be a winner, and that it paid to be smart and strong.

The SIP probation was one month. It was one more test to see if we could learn the skills needed to make it at

Scout Sniper School. After the thirty-day SIP (Sniper Indoctrination Program), I was sent to Quantico, Virginia, for the Scout Sniper Basic Course. I was extremely apprehensive on my way there but also excited to test myself. I wanted to learn as much as I could, and I felt ready. I arrived at the school anxious to learn the skills, and fully expecting to graduate.

One of the biggest differences between Marine Scout Snipers and other services snipers is our emphasis on being a Scout. Sniping is part of the job, but you must also master the 'scout' aspect of the work. To learn the 'scout' part meant communications, land navigation, patrolling, stalking, recon and surveillance. I thoroughly enjoyed it. We spent the entire school in the field, working in small teams. The training conditioned our minds; we were becoming hunters on the battlefield. It was an adjustment, my last deployment we patrolled roads, where we were the rolling targets.

We also learned to shoot with high-powered optics. I had used scopes to shoot wild game when I was younger and even had a small grasp on ballistics but, the education I received on optics and ballistics from these guys was phenomenal. The instructors were all seasoned veterans, most of whom had just come back from Iraq. I learned a lot from them and enjoyed the range time the most. However, my time in Quantico would only last a few weeks.

Unfortunately, I was injured on a conditioning run. The weight of a full ruck and a bad step tweaked my knee bad enough; for medical reasons, I was dropped from the course. I was heartbroken. The ride home was the longest ever. I'd never failed at anything, let alone something I wanted as bad as being a Marine Scout Sniper. For the first time, I realized that I wasn't Superman. I needed to learn much more. That's a hard pill to swallow for a young Marine with the wind at his back and strength on his side. Being humbled instilled in me the precise perspective I needed to become a sniper.

I returned to my Sniper Platoon expecting they'd drop me from the program. Thankfully, they decided to keep me. I like to think it was they knew I'd never quit, either way, I was glad they kept me. I began physical therapy while training for our upcoming deployment. Within months, I was back in shape, training, ready to jump on a boat for our unit's deployment.

26th MEU

Our battalion was part of the 26th Marine Expeditionary Unit (Special Operations Capable) or 26th MEU(SOC). It's not to say we were Special Operations Forces by any means. It simply meant we could conduct specialized amphibious, heliborne and mounted operations for the theater commanders as needed.

The training for a MEU is intense. As a Sergeant, I was a PIG, but still more senior than the rest of our team. I was made ATL (Assistant Team Leader). Much of our role would be R&S (reconnaissance and surveillance).

In February 2005, we finished our training work-up and boarded ships for our seven-month deployment. Our Scout Sniper Platoon was on the USS Kearsarge, an LHD (Landing Helicopter Dock) and the command deck for the BLT or Battalion Landing Team. We loaded our gear and equipment aboard our ship at Morehead City, NC. We were on our way to the Central Command's Theatre of Operations.

If you've never been on a ship, you're not missing much. Life is anything but enjoyable. We lived in cramped quarters, ate shitty food, and had little privacy. Your rack is the only getaway, but even then, there are people above you and below you, only a foot or so away. One positive outcome was not having much work to do. We mostly lifted weights, occasionally shooting our weapons off of the fantail of the boat.

It took about two weeks to get across the tumultuous Atlantic Ocean and into the Mediterranean Sea. We entered through the Straits of Gibraltar and sailed toward our first stop, Spain. There, we restocked supplies for the next leg of our trip. A small crew, with help from Marine Privates and Lance Corporals, loaded the supplies, and we were off to Israel.

Our Sniper Platoon was scheduled to cross-train with the Israeli Defense Force (IDF) for an annual two-week joint training operation. I wasn't complaining, it would be a nice break from the ship. When we arrived, our platoon separated from the Battalion. We met the IDF soldiers at their sniper and special operations compound training facility.

The Israelis are the utmost professionals and took pride in their craft. Love them or hate them, they know how to fight and how to win. They gained my full respect. The amount of real world experience they have is tremendous. Hell, they'd been fighting terrorists in their backyards for years. They gladly showed us a few tricks, some of which we'd use on later deployments. We especially enjoyed their ability to profile targets in counter-insurgency operations. Impressive.

The Israeli soldiers were great, and their facilities reflected realistic training environments. We shot on their ranges and trained alongside them, which eventually led to a culminating battalion level training operation to assault, clear, and hold an insurgent stronghold on one of the Israeli's training areas. The whole event was an excellent opportunity for all of us.

We re-boarded our ship and sailed for Greece. The USS Kearsarge docked in Rhodes, and we got a two-day liberty pass. That was our first, and only, overnight liberty port. Rhodes is an awesome little island; it had something for everyone. There were ancient artifacts and ruins along with old markets. It also had all the Mediterranean cuisine you could eat. Most notable our Marines and Sailors were the abundance of bars, of which we took full advantage.

I wish I could say I remembered my time on that beautiful island, but honestly, a good majority was a drunken blur. Dusty, our Platoon Corpsman, and I got shit faced for two days on Guinness and Irish car bombs. Naturally, this led to Dusty and another Marine, Tye, kicking the van of the Naval Fleet Commander or Commodore. They found themselves in trouble and standing tall before a Captain's Mast. They didn't care, the Commodore was an asshole, as were most of the Naval Officers.

Once our liberty in Greece ended, we drunken Marines and Sailors were rounded up, Herded onto the ship and set sail for Jordan, where another joint training exercise waited. However, this joint exercise would be totally different than the one with the Israelis. Unlike them, the Jordanians were not happy with our presence and wasted no time letting us know it.

We debarked ship and loaded vehicles for the ride to a desert training site. A few miles outside town, we learned our ship was attacked with rockets, forcing them to pull out of port. The Navy, God bless 'em, left the Marines from CAAT, who were providing security for them at the time, fending for themselves with no immediate backup or resupply. Luckily nobody was injured. Right then, I knew there was a reason we were issued security rounds.

Within hours, everything was clear, and we proceeded with the mission. Training with the Jordanians was hilarious. It was apparent, after observing them, they had no concept of discipline or marksmanship. The tactics we taught them were minimal, and as they tried executing them, we couldn't help but laugh at these grown men making idiots of themselves. It was priceless.

After a few weeks in Jordan, we said goodbye and good riddance. We floated through the Suez Canal, waved "hi" to our friends in Egypt, and headed to the Horn of Africa. Traveling through the Suez Canal was tough on the recon platoon and us snipers. Our task was providing early warning and precision fires against any threats, including the Somali pirates. They would have been utterly stupid to try anything against us. We manned the riggings on the mast of the ship with our weapons and optics. The Heat beat down the entire time making for a painfully blistering experience for all of us.

Once through the canal we stopped off the coast of Djibouti. A small ground force disembarked for training. Once the small ground force completed its joint training operations in the Horn of Africa, we headed back to sea and rounded the Arabian Peninsula, porting in Bahrain. After a quick resupply, we were back underway.

Our next port was the United Arab Emirates. The region was extravagantly elegant and surprisingly culturally diverse. We were allowed more liberty there, and a group of us visited a water park. It was strange seeing Muslim women in baroque's swimming next to European women in bikinis. In the wave pool, two little Arab girls appeared to be drowning. I helped them back to shore while nearly drowning myself. The little girls were happy to be alive, but their father wouldn't even acknowledge me, let alone thank me. I was surprised to learn that he was more upset that an infidel had touched his daughters than that they had almost died. That was my first of many cultural diversity experiences in the Arab world.

We again re-boarded the ship and sailed around the southern edge of the peninsula, steering toward the Gulf and Kuwait. We offloaded ship for a month of training in the Kuwaiti desert where we conducted multiple ranges. We even ran a short sniper competition at one range and did multiple long-range communication exercises and lots of patrolling. One thing we perfected, which would later prove to be useful, was desert hide training. That entailed mastering the art of building sites that would keep our sniper teams concealed in the harsh desert terrain. It was a must know skill for us.

Though it was miserable in Kuwait, we tried to have a good time. On one of the training exercises, we stayed in an old tent on a range. Josh, a known prankster, thought it would be fun to flip a big camel spider on Mateo. Mateo stood about 5'3" and weighed 240 pounds, all muscle. Josh set the trap and Mateo ran all of those 240 pounds right out of the tent, screaming like a school girl, when he realized the spider was on him. He later got out of the Corps and went on to play college football. But I'll never forget him as the big tough Teddy Bear.

During the work up for our deployment, Kayla became pregnant with our third child. She is my little princess Meghan. Born while we were out to sea, I wouldn't hold her until she was almost five months old. When I finally did, she's held my heart in her little hands ever since.

OIF III

Once our month of training was complete, we boarded the ship once more. I'm not sure why because a week later we offloaded and flew to Iraq in support of Operation Iraqi Freedom III.

On the first of June, the 26th MEU(SOC) split up and was sent to separate locations in the country, with two units even tasked with operations in Saudi Arabia. I was the assistant team leader (ATL) for Cherokee One. Our sniper team flew into Iraq via CH53 and linked up with a combined Australian and British force in the northern Muthanna province. Our base was south of Najaf, near a small town called Samawah.

Our mission in Samawah was strictly reconnaissance and surveillance. We punched out in four-man teams and split up into two two-man elements. Typically, we operated at night and collected intelligence on routes in and out of the city. The threat of IEDs made it vital that we kept tight observation.

Along the way, I realized that this was far different than my previous deployment with 2/8. I was no longer a moving target in a tin box waiting to get blown up. I was the dominant predator moving through the night.

Our team wanted action. Sitting on a ship wasn't our bread-and-butter, sniping was, and we hoped insurgents would show their faces. If they did, we were ready. I guess our aggressive posture didn't go unnoticed, and about a week later, the Australians started sending a chaperone with us to ensure we played nice. They were afraid, with good reason, that we might pick a fight.

After about a month in country, we headed back to Kuwait and through customs. Then it was back to the ships. You can image how frustrating it was for a bunch of snipers on a seven-month deployment with no real action. It wasn't like we craved combat, but it would have been nice to do our job. My mood improved, though, once I heard that I was given another chance at Sniper School in October, plus we learned the Battalion would be flying into Iraq next July.

It took us about a month to transit the Suez Canal once again. Once through, we stopped in Rhoda, Spain. I'm not positive, but Rhoda may have had a beer shortage shortly after we left, considering how much we all drank. After two days liberty, we climbed aboard the ship for the long voyage back across the Atlantic.

5 SCHOOL TRAINED

Second Chance

It's hard to explain arriving home again. I was finally able to see and hold my baby princess Meghan. Her little body in my arms softened my heart. I couldn't have spent enough time with her and my wife. Unfortunately, that joy was short lived. Five days after returning, I was back in Scout Sniper School, Stone Bay, on Camp Lejeune. This time around I was determined to graduate, no matter what.

I arrived at the basic sniper course knowing what to expect. The curriculum was exactly what you would think snipers need to know: land navigation, shooting, patrolling, stalking, and physical conditioning. I'd grown accustomed to pretty much all of it. I'd learned most of it on real world missions in Iraq. For me, it was just a matter of proving that I mastered the skills needed to become a Marine Scout Sniper.

The first few days back in school were administrative in nature, checking our rifles into the armory and getting settled in our barracks. We met our classmates, and it was obvious that all our nerves were on high. It was quite clear that everyone was anxious to get the show on the road. Among the class, those returning after having failed or being dropped were called Retreads. I was a Retread, dropped for medical reasons. That didn't matter to me; I was just thankful for the second chance

It pays to be a winner! That's the saying at Scout Sniper School, and if Marines grasp the concept right away, it can make life a little less miserable. The instructors drove that home each and every day during classes and during thrashings. It was a way to create competition as if we weren't competitive enough. Finishing first meant less pain, both physically and mentally. I adopted the saying as my mantra for the duration of sniper school.

As you can imagine, snipers are experts at the art of precision shooting. Just to get into the sniper platoon, you need to have qualified expert with the M16. At Sniper School, the basics are expanded upon, and we learned to engage targets in different shooting positions and from various ranges, for both stationary and moving targets. Our primary weapon was the M40A5, a free-floating, heavy barreled, bolt-action rifle we can use with a suppressor. My favorite part of using the weapon is the ability to pin-point a target and engage the enemy without warning or mercy.

Fieldcraft is another hallmark of Marine snipers, and one aspect is learning to patrol as a sniper team. Part of our mission is to move undetected into enemy terrain, and that means, knowing how to get in, set up, and get out. During school, our missions and patrols are under the watchful eye of the Instructors. It's nearly impossible to get over on them. They're all HOGs, and very seasoned. Usually, they've graduated top of their sniper class, completed multiple tours as a sniper, and know all the tricks in the book. I knew better than to attempt fooling them, but some Marines try cutting corners, but they don't usually last.

One of my favorite aspects of Sniper School was the amount of time we spent shooting on ranges. Loved to shoot. Not so much being physically thrashed. My favorite time though was taking "water samples" which meant running down to the point and jumping into the New River inlet to get a water sample for the Instructors. On the other hand, I truly hated running everywhere we went. I'm short with short legs, and the running kicked my ass! Thankfully my classmates were great guys and let me and my partner, who also hated running, be the students who were the advance party and 'arrived early'.

Along the way, we honed our observation skills with the use of various optics, and we also learned to operate new communication equipment. I can't stress enough the importance of communication. It was our lifeline to support, without it, teams cannot accomplish their missions.

We also learned how to adjust and control supporting arms and close air support. Mortars, artillery, helicopter, and fixed wing assets, all of which can save snipers at any time. Learning to coordinate these assets takes time and is a delicate process. Like many other things, the only way to learn this is to do it repeatedly, and during school that's exactly what we did.

One of the most important things we learned was applying camouflage. The necessity to blend, hide, and deceive is another hallmark trait of a sniper. Like shooting, it's one of the more famous aspects, and deservingly so. Blending into any environment in order to collect information and strike from the shadows is the bottom line for us. A great way to test a person's knowledge of this is stalking.

I learned to stalk through the painful personal application. We did it over and over, with the best snipers in the Corps observing, trying to catch us. In order to get a perfect score, a ten, you needed to move within 200 yards of the observer while setting up a shooting position. Then take two shots with your rifle, and begin your egress without being observed by the Instructors. Think of it this way. Imagine a grassy field. Now imagine two guys at one end with binoculars sitting in an elevated position while you're lying in the grass 1000 meters away. Your job is to sneak up on these guys, but remember, the men behind the bino's are school trained and experienced snipers themselves and know how to find other snipers. Sounds easy, right? Very tough.

In December 2005, I graduated Scout Sniper School. I had the highest grade point average and was awarded Honor Graduate for Class 1-06 at Stone Bay. I felt a weight lifted from my mind. I'd finally become a HOG. It was an accomplishment that so few know, and so few will ever achieve. For us in the sniper platoons, graduating the Basic Scout Sniper School allows us to get into more advanced sniper courses, which I was scheduled to attend.

After school, I returned to Second Battalion, Eighth Marines. I had earned the position of First Team Leader and Chief Scout Sniper, which meant I was the Senior Team Leader and Tactical Advisor to the Platoon Commander. I also had the secondary task of filling in for the Platoon Sergeant and ensuring the teams were properly trained. In the spring of 2006, Josh and I were sent to the Advanced Scout Sniper Course, also referred to as the Team Leaders Course. It's in Quantico at Scout Sniper Instructor School. The Advanced Course, now the Team Leaders Course, focused on advanced marksmanship, mission planning, and platoon training.

I enjoyed learning more about sniping. Knowing more meant having the ability to be more effective on the battlefield. It also meant that I would be more valuable. I took every opportunity to soak up information about my trade; that was my approach to every course.

The advanced course was a great experience. I met awesome individuals from all over the community and some from other branches of service and countries. I also ended up being the Honor Graduate for the class. I was asked to be an Instructor there when I returned from Iraq. I agreed, figuring Quantico would be a nice break for my family and an opportunity to get more training.

Spring turned into summer, and our departure grew closer to reality. After a trip to 29 Palms California for CAX (Combined Arms Exercise), we began packing. I moved Kayla and the kids up to Ohio and headed back down to Lejeune. On leave, I got some terrible news. The reality of being a sniper in combat came home. That June, in Ar Ramadi, Iraq, Corporal Reilly Baker from Missouri was killed. We had attended Sniper School together; he was a good man as well as a good sniper. Unfortunately, he was the first from class 1-06 killed in action.

OIF IV

In July 2006, our Battalion shipped off to Iraq once more. Jason, another team leader, and I went ahead of the Battalion to link up with the sniper platoon already there. We wanted them to paint us a picture, and provide an idea of the enemy's disposition. Jason and I hopped a C-17 cargo plane bound for TQ (Tal Quadim), Iraq. The plane stopped in Germany for fuel, then flew straight to TQ. From there, we jumped a ground convoy to Camp Fallujah. That's where we linked up with a team leader from First Battalion, First Marines Sniper Platoon (1/1) and headed to Karmah, along route Chicago.

Our new AO was in the infamous Al Anbar Province. From all accounts, I knew we were likely to see action. That was fine with me; I couldn't wait to get out and comb our new hunting grounds. It started just north of Fallujah and went east to Karmah. In Karmah, Jason and I conducted two missions with a team from 1/1, allowing us to see the lay of the land. One of the Sergeants, an ATL named Robinson, was a guy I instantly liked. We talked quite a bit; I was able to get to know him in a short time. Unfortunately, he was killed in Sangin, Afghanistan, some years later.

From Karmah, we headed back to Camp Fallujah. Our battalion took the responsibility of the Saq (Saqwaliyah) area spanning north of the train tracks in Fallujah and west to the Tartar canal. The region comprised of rural and built up cities. A vast arid wasteland dotted with small villages ran to the north, while the city of Karmah stretched east, with its urban sprawl and population of about 100,000. In the southwest of the AO, just above Fallujah proper, were the towns of Saqlawiyah and Shaddyville.

One company and one sniper team went west to reinforce Second Light Armored Reconnaissance Battalion (LAR) in Anah and Rawah, an area west of Ramadi. Our other four teams were in general support of the battalion. We primarily worked the Karmah and Saqlawiyah areas with Weapons and Golf Companies.

Our first week in country, John, my ATL, and I went to Saq to perform an area recon for the battalion commander, and the operations officer. I knew it would be a good chance for us to get a better look at the area, since First Battalion First Marines weren't able to inform us on it. No unit had a strong grasp of the area. Our battalion assumed responsibility for it in August after it being shuffled between two or three other units.

During the route recon in Saq, an IED blew a tire off our seven-ton truck. I felt lucky to survive another bomb blast. A family in a Ford Explorer also hit an IED that day. It blew the back off of their vehicle, amazingly; they escaped with minor injuries. We treated them the best we could, took a lot of pictures for HET (Human Exploitation Team), and moved on.

While we patrolled Saq, the other sniper teams went on missions with the sniper teams we were replacing from 1/1. The method was left-seat right-seat. During one of these missions, in the city of Karmah, the sniper teams sat in a hide located in an old hotel. It overlooked an area known as the lollipop, three roads intersected and formed a market. The road sign marking the area looked like a large metal lollipop. Somehow, during the night, insurgents managed to sneak under the team and toss a grenade up into their observation post (OP). Mike, the TL took shrapnel to the lung and spleen. Billy, the ATL, held security while Mike called in his own Cas-Evac (Casualty Evacuation) brief. I'm not sure what happened with the snipers from 1/1, but the

Marines from Weapons Company at the Iraqi police station pulled our wounded out.

Once the recon mission in Saq was complete, I briefed the battalion commander at Camp Fallujah. Right then, our sniper teams settled into a high paced operational tempo. One of our first tasks as a platoon was a counter mortar or POO (point of origin) mission. It was northwest of Saq, near a small parcel of land shaped like a triangle, but also surrounded by canals. From there, Insurgents were able to harass our positions with mortar fire. It was our job to find them. Unfortunately, the mission was unproductive, my point man Jeremy nearly went down with heat stroke. The desert sun was blazing hot. Good thing Dusty, our Doc, was nearby. He saved our bacon. Our dumbass Lieutenant should have listened to what we told him. The men needed to acclimate to the weather before pushing us out on a 96-hour operation during the first few weeks in country.

Weeks later, we were back in the triangle hunting for the mortar team again. This time, we set in on top the roof of a compound observing the area, when John and Jeremy saw something unusual. They noticed men who appeared to be setting an IED. One man in white held a bag while the other in blue was holding a shovel.

John and I prepared to fire. I adjusted my sights, in the heat of the moment; I got ahead of myself. I remembered the fundamentals and applied natural point of aim, allowing my sights to rest naturally on the man's chest. After a deep breath. I relaxed and focused on the reticle, on cue we both opened fire. To our surprise, our rounds fell short, hitting the dirt in front of the squatting men. Always double-check your range! That's a basic teaching that I'd overlooked. Lesson learned.

Johns MK11 (semi-automatic sniper rifle) jammed while the men stood up. My second round flew over the shoulder of the man in white as he began moving right to left. I chambered another round, and my third shot appeared to catch him on his left side, low in the abdomen. Not bad for a mover at 800 yards! The insurgent fell out of sight behind an embankment. The other man dropped his shovel and ran to the north. Shortly after, a pack of wild dogs sniffed after the man I'd shot. Apparently dogs could smell death in the air. We weren't able to confirm the kill. The squad that conducted the BDA (battle damage assessment) found a shovel, a small bag of bolts, and other metal objects used for fragmentation in IEDs.

On another mission in the Saq area, we identified two MAMs (military aged males) that appeared to be casing the area. They seemed very interested in the 'reed line' next to the road. We didn't have enough information to positively identify (PID) them as insurgents. We called higher ups and requested permission to engage based on enemy tactics, techniques, and procedures (TTPs) and our history of the area. Permission denied. The company sent out a squad to intercept and talk to the men. They denied everything, lied when confronted, and sent on their way. A week later, a patrol hit an IED in that exact Reed line. The Company

Commander burnt the vegetation to the ground and set up a platoon COP (Combat Outpost) in our old hide site.

Around that time, Golf Company decided to install a PB (patrol base) north of Route Mobile. It sat next to a village called Shadyville. It got its name because nothing good came from Shadyville. The whole damn area was "shady." One of our teams helped establish PB, and another joined shortly after. A week later, a Vehicle Bourne-IED (VBIED), specifically a fuel truck full of explosives, detonated at the entrance of the PB. Amazingly, no Marine KIA, but many wounded. The blast was so strong it destroyed the exterior walls and a seven-ton truck parked in front of the compound. The damage was such that Golf Company had to abandon the Patrol Base.

After the VBIED attack, enemy activity in Saq increased, as if there wasn't enough already. In particular, there were more attacks from enemy snipers and designated marksmen. It appeared that a fairly accurate designated marksman (DM) had come to play. A few Marines experienced close calls, being shot in their armored chest and back plates and Kevlar helmets.

By September, the violence escalated rapidly. Squads continuously took fire. That month, Lance Corporal March was killed by the marksman. Around the same time, Chris, one of Golf Companies squad leaders, lost his legs to an IED. My team headed to Saq looking to eliminate the enemy sniper. We also needed to gather information for the CI/HUMINT (Counter-Intelligence/Human Intelligence)

Marine named Mac. He specialized in interrogations, information collection, and translation among other things. Helping us sort out the who's who in the area is what he aimed to do. That helped us locate targets more systematically.

Before I left, I told Nick, one of Golf Company's squad leaders, I would get the enemy sniper who killed March. I lived to regret that promise. In hindsight, I wish I could have known the outcome of things. Being unable to keep that promise cost a good Marine his life. I'm thankful for the time and opportunity to get to know Nick and the rest of the guys from Golf Company.

From the start, October 6, 2006, was a disastrous day. Golf Company planned March's Memorial while Stephen's squad left on patrol at noon. Stephen sent his Marines to prepare the vehicles while he went to the COC (Command Operations Center) to turn in his patrol manifest. He heard a single gunshot and ran outside. One of his SAW gunners negligently discharged his weapon, a stupid boot mistake. While loading the weapon, he rode the bolt home with rounds on the feed tray. He was issued a proper ass chewing and sent to the Lieutenant. The Officer gave him the "shit happens, you need to learn and grow from it" speech.

Stephen double-checked his men to ensure they were ready. Everything was good, except their personal radios stopped working. Since they were more of a luxury than a necessity, the squad switched the truck order and decided to use hand and arm signals to communicate between the turret gunners.

Problem solved; the squad hit the road and headed through Saq. They drove north on Route Lobster and set up a Snap VCP, (vehicle checkpoint) just outside of town. When finished, they continued towards the Trout Canal and the Go Army Bridge. Earlier, the LT told Stephen the Captain and his PSD (Personal Security Detachment) traveled over the bridge to First Platoon's area. He told him if he wanted, to sweep the road north of the bridge for IED'S before the Captain came back that way.

Stephen stopped his patrol short of the bridge, then decided to cross. His truck went first, then the second truck, followed by the high back. As they turned left onto a long stretch of road, he heard a pop. It didn't seem loud, but his driver pulled off the road and turned, stretching to see what happened. Fire and smoke billowed from a vehicle they didn't recognize. It took a second to realize the truck had absorbed the full brunt of a massive IED. Instantly, his Marines reacted, dismounting to search for secondary bombs. Something on the ground caught Stephen's eye. It was his squad member Payne laying face up a few feet away. He was dead. His body was intact but unrecognizable.

Near the blazing vehicle, another Marine limped from the wreckage. Rather than wait for the area cleared, Stephen said fuck it, as he ran to the vehicle looking for survivors. As he ran, all hell broke loose. The IED initiated ambush worked like a charm, trapping his squad in the kill zone.

Small arms fire streaked in from three directions. Bullets drilled holes in the vehicles and whizzed overhead, but the Marines fought back. Machine gunners in the gun turrets ferociously returned fire, while Team Leaders established covering positions directing their team's return fire.

As Stephen reached the wreckage, he found Hale unconscious and still inside the burning vehicle. The smoldering fire was too hot to pull him out. Several Marines tried retrieving him until Stephen ordered them to get the water coolers from the trucks. They returned, dumping ice water inside the vehicle as others pulled Hale out. As if it couldn't get worse, one of their vehicle radios was destroyed, the other two wouldn't work. With the radio's down, Stephen popped red flares signaling their distress and loss of communication assets. His men continued fighting back the ambush. It didn't take long, they gained fire superiority and repelled the ambush enough to begin safely evacuating the dead and wounded. As the situation calmed, Stephen quickly accounted for his men. He and realized the turret gunner from the destroyed vehicle, Johnson, was missing. Stephen organized what was left of his squad, preparing for an evacuation.

The blast instantly killed Johnson, Payne, and the Iraqi interpreter. Hale and another Marine, Reagansburg, were severely burned, with Hale being the worst of the two. I was back at the FOB's COC when the ambush went down. I remember the casualties arriving. Our platoon Doc, Dusty, did his best to help save them both, but only one survived.

Hale died, pronounced dead when the bird landed at the TQ. Just last night, I'd asked Hale to come out for selection when we got home. It's a shame we lost such a great kid.

Billy's Team and mine provided over watch as divers searched the river for Johnson's body. Turns out he was launched into the canal by the blast, along with part of the vehicle. Divers took turns searching for his remains underwater. It took three days before they found him.

After the catastrophe at Saq, my team was tasked with a reconnaissance and surveillance mission. The area of interest was south of us, and we were to identify HVTs and the traffic patterns on the routes to and from our river crossings. The information went to the intelligence section, Mac the HUMINT guy, the infantry companies, and other agencies. That helped us to conduct raids on the asshole insurgents while they slept. The process worked well. We provided pictures while the squads brought other information, which allowed Mac to connect the dots on the insurgent cells and relationships in the area.

Once again, we tried counter sniper operations in the area, but with no luck. The operations only provided more intel but no dead enemy snipers. That was very frustrating.

By mid-October, the Battalion Operations Officer tasked our platoon with hunting down and eliminating the IED cell in the Saq area. They were the same ones responsible for the actions on the Go Army Bridge and the catastrophic IED on my friend's squad. We were more than happy to help.

The LT, Chris, and I formulated a plan. My team along with two other teams would conduct constant surveillance, and counter-IED (C-IED) missions in the vicinity of the bridge until the enemy appeared. Rotating shifts of twenty-four hours on and forty-eight hours off would continue until we stopped the IED cell for good. For two and a half weeks, we took turns watching the bridge. While extracting from one of these missions, the squad supporting us was called as the QRF (Quick Reaction Force) for an Iraqi Police Station. It was under attack again. My team had no choice but to tag along. We pulled around to the IP (Iraqi Police) station; insurgents were busy exchanging gunfire. A squad of policemen tried falling back to the compound.

"Upfront! an IP is down in the street!" I heard. Nichols, our Marine squad leader, looked confused. Clearly, he didn't know what to do. "My team and I will dismount. Doc's coming with us," I yelled to Nichols. We jumped from our vehicles moving quickly to the policeman. My teammates, John, and Jeremy, covered Doc and me as we stripped off the IP's armor. We pulled his uniform back and knew he wouldn't make it. We looked at each other, we both knew. Doc said, "The bullet entered his heart." He bled out and died in front of us. There was nothing we could do. Jeremy came forward, he and I dragged his body out of the street and into the IP station. We headed back to our vehicles, loaded up and drove back to Golf Company's CP (Command Post) at the Hotel California. Then and there, I realized death doesn't care who you are or what side you're fighting on. Bullets have no conscience, in combat anyone could be struck down at any moment.

Finally, on November 10, 2006, we brought a small taste of justice for the men of Golf Company. Our sniper teams kept hunting the insurgent cell responsible for the attack on Stephen's squad. Our big problem was using the same hides. We were setting a pattern that could cost us dearly. We needed different hides, but current sniper doctrine insisted we keep a certain distance between our site and the possible target location. Then, John came up with an idea I liked, so we went for it.

We abandoned the long-range approach and hid in the reeds along the canal, approximately 15 yards from the road. We stripped off our normal gear and wore our ghillie suits to blend in. We chose our M4's, leaving our sniper rifles behind because we were so close to the targets. It was an extremely risky choice. If compromised, we'd be vulnerable. But it was a chance we were willing to take. In the end, it paid off.

We moved into position late one night, waiting for sunrise. At first light, an old man walked to the bridge. I'd seen him before and reported his activity to higher ups. To me, I knew he was a lookout. He wasn't a threat, just a pawn. Insurgents liked to use old men, women, and children to act as scouts and human shields. Still, the fact remained he was participating in the act of trying to kill my brothers. Looking back, part of me regrets not killing that old bastard on principal alone.

Around midday, John positively ID'd a man digging in the road. He was near the bridge and only 15-20 yards away. He said, "Joe, this guy needs to die." Time to start the party. Two more insurgents, one by the trunk of the car parked nearby, and one standing by the driver's door, were nearby. Because of the angle, the vehicle slightly protected both men from us. In seconds, my team was ready for the kill, but like an idiot, I didn't designate targets. I should have assigned each member a person to shoot.

I initiated the ambush with a ten round burst. Mr. Ganush's chest and liver took all ten rounds in about a five-inch group. My other Marines opened up, wounding the two wounded insurgents by the car, and they fled down the bank of the nearby river.

There was no return fire, so we quickly combed the area. I left Jeremy and John on security while Matt and I swept the kill zone. Mr. Ganush lay on top the IED like he'd been praying to his Mother or Allah. For his effort in trying to kill us, we rewarded him with simultaneous headshots from Matt and me. Up close and personal. Our rounds removed half his face, and it couldn't have happened to a nicer guy.

Once the QRF appeared, we tried tracking the other two, with no success. Later, Mac radioed that two bodies were found in an abandoned pump house by the Euphrates only a few hundred meters from our ambush site. Word spread quickly, and the Marines of Golf Company cheered at the news we'd finally got those responsible for the IEDs. It happened on November 10, the Marine Corps Birthday. Without a doubt, the best Marine Corps Birthday I've ever experienced.

It was around this time; nearly all the Iraqi Army forces in Karmah had either been killed or deserted. Weapons Company was left with nothing but a handful of Iraqi Police and the all but useless Iraqi Army, or what was left of it, to contain the city. Karmah was then declared as one of the most deadly cities in all of Iraq; a real hot vacation spot.

Insurgents attacked coalition forces on a daily basis. They also embarked on a thorough murder and intimidation campaign aimed at the locals. There methods? They'd kill any Iraqi Policeman they could get their hands on, and any local who helped US forces.

One day, Weapons Company conducted a snap VCP. They detained a man who'd been driving around with another man's head in the back of his car. The head apparently belonged to his cousin and had been cut off as a punishment for dishonoring the family name. We joked it was a hard life; he was doing what he had to do to get ahead!

On November 24, our sniper platoon came together on Camp Fallujah for a few days of rest. We sat around bullshitting, when Doc Narvaez burst into the room, "Nick's been shot!" All we knew he'd been in the IP station in Saq. It was a shock, but since he was en route to TQ, and we had limited information, I assumed he'd be okay.

A few hours later Doc returned, Nick died. It was a somber night and morning. My team packed and headed back to Golf Company's AO. I talked to Mikey, one of the riflemen in Nick's squad. He explained that Nick was opening the gate to the IP station; as he did a sniper struck him with a round to the throat. His squad immediately tossed a smoke grenade to shield the downed Marine while returning fire. Other Marines tried saving their brother's life. I couldn't deny my sadness and frustration. The enemy sniper had gotten to Nick before I could get to him.

We held a Memorial Service for Nick, then began working reconnaissance and ambush missions in the hope of killing more insurgents and the enemy sniper. The missions were tedious and tiresome. We used our cameras and took pictures rather than pulling triggers. On one mission, we snuck on the roof of a fully occupied house, using it for an operational OP for over a day before being discovered. The next evening a young boy came up on the roof to feed his pigeons and almost shit himself at the sight of us.

Later, we conducted an extremely long mission near a place known as the Japanese Bridge on the Tartar Canal. We never caught the IED cell, but after five agonizing days of lying in a ditch in the desert sun, we all came close to losing minds. On the fifth and final night, we were bored, and someone decided to put a lonely, starving, stray donkey out of its misery. The old donkey was one tough, loud old bastard. I ended up having to put 7.62mm round in his head to help him understand it was time to die.

A short time later, we were called on to provide support for a raid on an insurgent hotspot. We would provide reconnaissance and surveillance for the grunts doing the door kicking. We'd go in a day early, scope out the terrain and the enemy's patterns and relay to the grunts. To find a position for the mission, we'd need to infiltrate the target area from north of Fallujah, near the train station.

A day later, after finishing briefings and rehearsals, we settled down for a bit of rest. It was late evening, and my morning chow was knocking on my back door, demanding an exit. I went over to the all too familiar Iraqi port-a-shitters for a stinky visit. While dropping a few pounds in the putrid mess, all hell broke loose outside.

The night lit up as our outpost took incoming small arms and medium machine gun fire. I was confused. How do I react? Still sitting on the shitter with my pants down, I looked up to see shafts of light perforating the port-a-shitter above my head. The top of the outhouse was in some assholes PKM cone of fire. I'm stumped on what to do. I can't stand up and didn't want to go out of the shitter with my pants down. So I finished my business, waited for the asshole to quit shooting and went outside.

Things settled down after my fireworks in the shitter. We kept on the mission and patrolled to our objective area. Once there, we set up our observation post, watching our target building for 24 hours. The raid force stormed in and captured people without a fight. They segregated every MAM (Military Age Male) in the compounds and questioned them. It turned out it was a good op, thirteen of the MAM's were Al Qaeda assholes. Our Marines also rescued three Iraqi hostages, making the operation a great success.

With the successful Op behind us, we went to work in Karmah, Iraq. In theory, the unit we relieved had given the city back to the Iraqi Army and Iraqi Police, except for a few patrol bases along route Chicago. Assuming the Iraqi's could or would hold their own was assuming a lot. Weapons Company would have less than 100 men from our Weapons Company to keep route Chicago free of IEDs. They were also expected to provide a QRF for SOF units, the Iraqi Army, and Iraqi Police. A tall order for a unit with such limited numbers.

By December, only a handful of Iraqi Army and Police were left in Karmah. Most were killed or abandoned their posts. Among them sat Weapons Company, who tried assisting them while squaring off against insurgents running rampant in a city we weren't allowed to enter. Insurgents intimately knew our AO boundaries and used the lack of Iraqi Police presence to their advantage, partly due to the lack of Iraqi Army presence. None of them were safe in Karmah.

Three of our sniper teams arrived in mid-December. It was like pulling teeth to get permission from the battalion for us to do our jobs. Even when we were allowed, operating in the heart of the city was off limits. The risk of us being outnumbered was too great. Because of that policy, we decided to concentrate our efforts along route Chicago, the Iraqi Police Station, and the market near the Lollipop.

Insurgents were wreaking havoc on the Iraqi Police, attacking their station daily. The undermanned police couldn't stop the incoming small arms, RPG, and mortars. The bad guys dialed their mortars in well. During one attack, a round blew apart our Marine berthing area. One mortar landed right in the middle of the open courtyard, at the center of the IP station. Luckily, the Marines were patrolling. The stupid insurgents forgot to pull the safety pin from the mortar, and it wouldn't have hurt anyone had they been there.

When attacks came on the IP station, my men went to the high ground. Elevated positions allowed us better target acquisition. But to get to the high ground meant running a gantlet of lead. During one attack, Chris and I were at Post One talking to our Marines watching the Lollipop area and an old hotel. We learned we could anticipate attacks by watching locals in the market. If the market cleared, it was a bad sign, and that's just what happened.

When the shooting started, I began observing the hotel. Through my scope, I noticed a shadow followed by a flash. Some asshole sent a few rounds our way. I put a bullet through his window and moved to find a better position. Being under attack, I ran to a pile of rubble as a few Marines with M203 grenade launchers followed. I directed their fire down an alleyway where the enemy was maneuvering to get in position and take sporadic shots at the IP station. Atop the rubble, I noticed an old broken down building across the street with multiple loopholes in it. From there amidst the rubble, I shot into the loopholes of the buildings we were receiving fire. Any hole I noticed a muzzle flash coming from, I put a bullet.

When the firefight stopped, I looked around and realized that I had no cover. Not smart, especially during a firefight. How I managed to make it through the twenty-minute chaos unscathed is a miracle.

Another time, a very successful mission for us in Karmah was a "bait and switch" ambush. The idea was to goad the enemy into attacking one of our team's fake positions while other teams ambushed the attacking insurgents from another position.

During one mission, my team holed up in a school covering another team, just across the street. The fake position was nearby. Our intended ambush worked brilliantly, almost. Instead of attacking the decoy position, insurgents attacked an Iraqi Police station not too far from us, and from an angle that allowed the other sniper team to open fire. Billy, the team leader, whacked three or four insurgents before all hell broke loose in the city. Civilians rushed from the market as insurgents moved in for the attack. Approximately fifty civilians crowded into the courtyard below us putting my team in one hell of a predicament.

During the chaos of fighting, we spotted three Iraqi's in the street examining the approaching QRF vehicles. In retrospect, we should have taken them out. Their body language and mannerisms left us thinking they probably orchestrated the attack. They fit the profile of insurgents, but we couldn't positively identify them as targets because of their lack of weapons. I now regret not killing them.

With the QRF en route, our teams collapsed for extract. Our problem was bypassing the crowd in the courtyard; we needed to disperse them. Two flash-bangs did the trick. While their ears rang, we dashed into the street running to the hotel where the other team was waiting. We expected to see the mounted armor of HMMV's as our QRF pulled up. But they didn't cover us, they weren't there, an IED took them out on the way to our position. We were on our own. Once at the hotel we linked up with Billy's team. Our only choice? We'd run the "Mogadishu Mile" with cover fire from the posts inside the IP station. It was a long five hundred meters to the Iraqi Police entrance and safety. Later that day, insurgents tried a retaliatory attack on the police station. Billy put down a couple more bad guys for good measure.

After Karmah, my team transitioned back to Saq. We spent most of our efforts on reconnaissance and surveillance, along with a few counter-IED missions. During one mission, we set up along a route running through a small market on the west side of town. To allow for more coverage, we split our teams. I put three of my guys into the reeds along the road opposite the market, while John and I settled into an old broken down, abandoned house about seventy-five meters down the road. The operation was a complete bore due to lack of enemy activity, when Matt radioed us, "We got a crowd of shady dudes over here." He didn't have PID that they were bad so we couldn't do a thing. Ever resourceful, Matt asked permission to conduct a

"Psychological Operation" on the group. "Sure, why not?" I replied. He shot a dog in the middle of the group using his suppressed M4. The dog went ballistic, flopping all over the ground while the men scattered like cockroaches, probably praying that Allah would save them. It took all I had to not laugh out loud on the rooftop where we sat. On that deployment, I witnessed an unbelievable event. A squad of Marines from Cherokee Five videotaped the rape of a donkey! Yes, a donkey. The video was both disturbing and hilarious. I thought things like that were propaganda rumors spread by our troops, but I was wrong. Who knew that Iraqi men really fuck donkeys?

Around the time of the donkey episode, Marines from Golf Company, with help from Mac, the Intel guy, finally nabbed the enemy sniper working in the area. To this day, I'm still pissed I wasn't able to catch him in the act and kill him myself. I can only hope all of our work as snipers, gathering intel and taking photos, contributed to the capture of that bastard. Who knows how many Marines he killed, including my friend Nick? For that, I hoped he died a painful death at the hands of the Iraqi Police. I know for sure he took a 'fall' down some steps en route to the detention facility.

Jason's team took part in a successful mission about the same time. He hid along the Euphrates River conducting surveillance, when they intercepted four insurgents trafficking weapons and supplies up the river in a boat. The men had no idea they were there. Jason's snipers initiated the ambush with a claymore mine, then unloaded M203 grenades and small arms fire into them. The snipers were on the riverbank, directly broadside of the boat from thirty yards. The insurgents had no chance of making the shore. Their bodies drifted down the river, leaving their sinking boat.

One of our last missions in Saq, we dubbed the "Grenade House Mission." My team crept into a shitty neighborhood, took over a house we'd previously used. Unbeknownst to us, someone in the local militia found our footprints leading into the house. They also spotted our periscopes from the rooftop. The militia sent an old man with a young male, both sporting pistols, to inspect our hide site. We understood they thought we might be insurgents. That's why they were probing our building, but we weren't about to let them in.

The two men approached very cautiously. Something about their disposition and attitude made us nervous. We decided not to mow them down. Maybe it was our strict

ROEs? They did have weapons; technically it would have been legit to drop them. We also took into account Golf Company had been trying hard to assist the militia in this area. We decided as long as they didn't try to breach our building, they'd live. Hell, they may even draw out some insurgents for us.

We tried waving them off, undeterred; they tried entering through a barricaded door on the first floor. Enough is enough. We rolled two M67 fragmentation grenades down the steps. The door apparently shielded them from the blast because miraculously they lived, running into a nearby house. With the help of the QRF team, we detained the young man and confirmed he was indeed part of the local militia.

Finally, the day came to leave Iraq, and our platoon did a relief in place with my buddy Paul's platoon from 2/7 from California. It was a good RIP. One of their first missions with us, they shot a couple of insurgents across the Euphrates River. It was a good start for them and their deployment.

By the end of February, our entire Battalion consolidated to Camp Fallujah to begin the trip home. We convoyed to TQ, flew down to Kuwait where we patiently negotiated through customs. With quick refuel in Germany, and several hours in the air we were home.

It was always great to come home. I enjoyed the reunion with my family and friends. As always, my wife and kids were there to greet me, but with each deployment I could feel a piece of me stayed in the war zone. My heart and mind remained with my fallen brothers in Iraq. Our Battalion lost nine Marines killed in action. The Battalion also suffered twenty percent casualties. Twenty percent of your troops wounded in combat equals a lot of fucked up men, and back then they weren't handing out Purple Hearts for concussions or sprained ankles. That's close to 200 Marines who sacrificed their blood and bodies in the Al Anbar Province of Iraq.

I needed a break. I took the Instructors in Quantico up on their offer to work with them. I moved to Virginia in April of 2007 to start a new chapter in my education as a sniper. I would be at the Scout Sniper Instructor School.

6 TEACHING TO FIGHTING

Instructing

I felt honored checking into Weapons Field Training Battalion as an Instructor at the Scout/Sniper Instructor School in Quantico, Virginia. The idea of teaching others what I'd learned, and the possibility of that information saving lives, was worth the experience alone. Also, I knew that it would only benefit my learning as well.

At the Scout/Sniper Instructor School, we taught not only the Scout/Sniper Basic Course, but also the Advanced Team Leader Course, and the Scout/Sniper Unit Leaders Course. The latter was only for the Team Leaders, Chief Scouts, Platoon Sergeants, and Platoon Commanders. Until then, my experience was at the team level, but by the time I finished instructing, I understood the in-depth role of snipers and their deployment.

I quickly settled into my new position and received formal training such as teaching, speaking, and platform instruction. The difference between the work of sniping and the work of instructing was immediately apparent. I needed to learn the art of Power Points and keystrokes rather than rapid bolt manipulation and formulating wind-calls.

Teaching added to my knowledge of sniping and sniper employment. While at the schoolhouse, I had time to dissect the curriculum and digest the lessons. I examined my experiences along with that of the staff and students, most of whom had been down range in some capacity before attending the courses. My study and instructing sharpened my proficiency in tactics and further developed my knowledge of the battlefield.

Initially, I took charge of teaching miscellaneous field skills and led the instruction of mission planning. I also taught land navigation, communications, and was a secondary instructor on marksmanship. Fortunately, after about six months, I completely took the reins as lead on marksmanship for all courses. That suited me just fine. An excellent fit, since I'd enjoyed shooting for as far back as I could remember.

The Basic Course meant long hours on the range. The reward was turning sub-par or average shooters into professionals able to consistently hit targets at 1,000 yards (914 meters) with the M40, a 7.62mm caliber sniper rifle. While teaching marksmanship, I continued to help with field skills and mission planning. Being able to teach and instruct in all aspects of sniping and sniper employment undoubtedly made me a more knowledgeable scout/sniper and leader.

Eventually, I received a Master Instructor Certification. I met the requirements set by the Marine Corps, putting in the required 2,000 hours. I attained the distinction as an expert in the subject of sniping and sniper employment. Through it all, I kept in mind that being an instructor did not mean that I couldn't learn from students or the other staff, and often that's just what happened. Many of the students just returned from Iraq or Afghanistan and updated us instructors, on new successful and unsuccessful enemy and friendly tactics, techniques, and procedures.

The people I met at Quantico were remarkable, students and staff. While there I was able to network, while having a direct influence on the scout/sniper community. Because I knew I'd eventually reenter the Fleet, I kept an eye out for stellar Marines I'd later hope to recruit for my platoon. Two such men I met were Rob and Mac, who I took to Afghanistan in 2011.

When we weren't fielding classes, we attended other courses. I attended several, including Urban Sniper, an excellent precision shooting and urban employment course, and High-Risk Personnel, which was one of the most enjoyable courses. There, in one week, we shot thousands of rounds through our pistols. Foreign Weapons Instructor course informed us on and allowed for hands-on with various foreign weapons systems. SERE (Survival, Evasion, Recovery, and Escape) was an experience in itself. Nothing like getting your ass beat by a giant SEAL to give you a wake-up call. I also managed to complete my Associate's Degree. and had the first of two back surgeries.

Another great aspect of instructing was time spent with family. Although we worked tons of hours, I was home most nights, which was a big change for my wife and kids. It was during this time I had the first of two back surgeries. I also witnessed the birth of my youngest son Nicholas, at Bethesda Naval Hospital. We named him after Corporal Nicholas Paul Rapavi, one of the best Marines I've known. He was one of the best squad leaders of Golf Company 2/8, a true leader, and a good friend. I didn't know Nick well until that deployment, when our team began working with his company and squad. I quickly learned he and his Marines were as reliable as any and they'd risk their lives to pull our ass out of a mess, come hell or high water. My little Nick is definitely his father's son. It's amazing and frightening, how much he looks and acts like his old man. It's my hope and fear he too will be a killer someday.

Although my family and I thoroughly enjoyed our time at Quantico, come summer of 2010, it was time to leave. I'd been there over three years. That July, my family picked up and moved once again. My orders were to Camp Lejeune, North Carolina; I joined the 3d Battalion, 2nd Marine Regiment's Scout/Sniper Platoon.

Our Platoon

On arrival, the Battalion Commander, Lt. Col. Dixon, selected me as the Scout/Sniper Platoon Commander. He thought it better to fill the billet with a former instructor of the Scout/Sniper Unit Leaders Course than an inexperienced Officer. I was in the unique position of being the Platoon Commander instead of the Platoon Sergeant. That fell to a junior Staff Sergeant named Brandon.

I was grateful to be Platoon Commander, and with that responsibility, I set out to build the best scout/sniper platoon in the Marine Corps. I did it with the help and support of my Platoon Sergeant and the Battalion and Company staffs. Unfortunately, the starting point wasn't good. The Platoon's reputation wasn't stellar in the Battalion or the sniper community. When I arrived, the platoon had fourteen men and only one school trained scout/sniper or HOG. The men knew my reputation, and I knew a few of them from previous assignments or my work as an instructor.

After a talk with the Battalion Commander, my Platoon Sergeant Brandon and I, set out to fill the ranks of our platoon. We developed an in-depth training schedule, then an indoctrination/selection program to build the platoon to full strength. To the Battalion Commander, full strength was a forty plus man platoon. He wanted a platoon that could cover a large Area of Operations in Afghanistan. The one we intended to receive. He wanted a strong platoon that could beat back the Taliban still controlling a majority of our intended area. If we succeeded, it would allow the line companies to concentrate on interacting with the locals and conducting training and stabilization operations. That meant holding more selections to open the doors for Marines wanting to become snipers. We'd held one, but I set up one more two-week selection and filled the platoon with hard-charging infantrymen putting us near the numbers we needed.

Meanwhile, I recruited as many experienced HOGs as I could. More school-trained snipers allowed us to build longevity into the platoon and ensured that we had the experience needed in key leadership positions. I was happy to get Rob and Mac, two Marines from 1/6 I'd put through the basic course in Quantico. I was able to snag a west coast sniper, Nate, who came highly recommended by the instructors out west.

It wasn't long til' we found out for sure Afghanistan was our destination. With the news, I made it a point to begin training as soon as possible. Some of our snipers had been to Afghanistan, we knew what to expect. For those who hadn't been, I tried creating an environment as nearly resembling Afghanistan as I could. We trained and held exercise around Camp Lejeune, Fort Pickett, Virginia, and 29 Palms, California. Much of our focus was spent reiterating individual, team, and platoon level tasks. We also worked on learning to support company, battalion, and regimental operations.

We also fired a lot of ammunition. We shot multiple known distance ranges, allowing the Marines to collect data on their weapons systems, along with unknown distance ranges. We used the unknown distance shoots for drills teaching the Marines rapid target engagements using holds and leads in their scopes while incorporating moving targets as well. We also drilled immediate actions with our M4s over and over and over, until the men knew instinctually, without question or thinking, how to react in any situation or during contact with the enemy.

On the administrative side, getting my men seats to Sniper School wasn't a problem. We sent sixteen Marines to the basic course during that time, and fifteen graduated from Quantico and Stone Bay. Five graduated with honors.

If not in schools, my Marines were training, training, and training. The old adage practice makes perfect applies for snipers as well. Mastering basic and advanced infantry skills like patrolling and small unit tactics was fundamental, as was conducting sniper specific missions such as supporting other units and acting as the main effort. Over time, the hard work resulted in teams of snipers that thought and acted collectively as one without any hesitation.

I'm sure at times my men hated me for making them constantly repeat immediate action drills, interdict targets, and the endless hours of patrolling. There was a method to the madness. In combat, Marines need to react to enemy fire and all other dangers immediately while making split second, life-changing decisions. That's the reason for the countless hours of repetition and the building of what the military likes to call 'muscle memory.' In the end, all the pain and suffering and the rounds put down range developed the most accomplished and well-trained scout/sniper platoon the Marine Corps had seen in a very long time.

The platoon received rave reviews from the Battalion and Regimental staffs as well as the official evaluators at 29 Palms MAGTF (Marine Air Ground Task Force) Combined Arms Exercise personnel. Our platoon received the highest scores of any sniper platoon to date, the fall of 2010. The Command, my Platoon Sergeant, and I accomplished the goal of developing a large, well-trained platoon of snipers. We consisted of thirty-nine Marines and two sailors. Twenty-three of the Marines were school trained HOGs, and the others were hand selected, exceptional infantrymen.

I believe we assembled, trained and developed the best scout/ sniper platoon the Corps had ever conceived. A grand statement I know, but in time, the success of our Platoon and the praise we received seemed to validate that idea. On countless occasions, and from sources such as the Coyotes (Training Evaluators) of 29 Palms, and to Generals, our Sniper Platoon was applauded for excellence displayed in training and combat.

By January 2011, the training tempo slowed as we prepared to deploy. The break allowed the Marines to take care of last minute paperwork and ensure their affairs were in order. During this time, our Platoon suffered its first setback. My Platoon Sergeant and fellow scout/sniper had a nervous breakdown that ended in a standoff with the Jacksonville North Carolina SWAT Team. He was admitted to the fourth floor Psych Ward of the local Naval Hospital. Needless to say, Brandon didn't deploy with us. He stayed back to get his head right and take care of his family. In turn, we received a new Platoon Sergeant, Edward Deptola.

Dep, as I called him, had been with a sniper platoon in 2d Battalion, 2d Marine Regiment. He'd also attended Sniper School, but failed during stalking phase. Since he was the only available Staff Non-commissioned Officer in the Battalion with relative experience, he was the obvious choice, even if he was a PIG.

In retrospect, Dep turned out to be God sent. He was not only a true gunfighter at heart, his touch of OCD gave him extraordinary organizational skills, which helped us immensely. We also complimented each other's personality and leadership styles perfectly. He was relaxed, with an excellent sense of humor and a twisted mindset like mine. He found humor in just about every situation. I critiqued and seriously analyzed everything, but also had a sense of humor, even if it was a dark, and sadistic one.

The Authors Assistant Team Leader, John
Observing with a Periscope

Matt Halle - A sniper in the Author's Team
Picture taken north of Fallujah, near Saqlawiyah, Iraq - 2006

OP Riviera in Saqlawiyah, Iraq.
G Co 2/8 Company FOB just north of Fallujah.

The Author - December 2006 - Karmah, Iraq

Sniper Team - Reaper 1 - Afghanistan

Doc Vauss - Corpsman - Afghanistan 2003/04

Sniper Team - Reaper 2 - Afghanistan

Moks - The Author's Gunner
Afghanistan 2003/04

Sniper Team - Reaper 3 - Afghanistan

Reaper 4 in Action - 2011 Afghanistan

Sniper Team - Reaper 4 - Afghanistan

The Author (L) with Rob Richards (R) - Afghanistan

Sniper Team - Reaper 5 - Afghanistan

The Author in Action - July 2011 - Afghanistan

7 THE FRAY

Deployed

At the end of training and leave, our Battalion set off on deployment. Our first team left for Afghanistan in February of 2011 while the rest of us shipped off on March 1. Before we left, our families gathered to say our last goodbyes. I offered words of encouragement and told many of the wives and Mothers not to worry, "I'll bring the guys home safe." I honestly believed I could, but I should have known better than to think I could keep a promise of that magnitude.

In transit, we enjoyed a short layover in a quaint hotel in Ireland. It was nice spending a few days in the lush green hills. Experience told me that Irelands surreal atmosphere would be the last bit of peace we'd encounter for some time to come. I soaked it up. Before I knew it, we landed in chilly Kyrgyzstan. It had definitely changed since my first trip there in 2003. It was now a formal US Air Base with everything you could want. We ended up spending a week, waiting for a flight to southern Afghanistan.

Our day came, and we headed for the Helmand Province and Camp Leatherneck, or "Pleasureneck" as we infantry types called it. The name was a poke at the POGs (Personnel Other than Grunts) who lived the good life on base while we got our asses shot off. Sadly, they rate the same pay as we do. From my experience, they were usually the guys in the bar telling war stories. The reality? They lived exclusively on a protected base with no enemy contact.

My return to Afghanistan felt almost like a homecoming. As strange as it sounds, I took comfort in the simplicity of life in a combat zone. We were there strictly to hunt down and kill Taliban and insurgents in their dirty wonderland. The best part, now I had a whole platoon of killers ready to make that happen.

I felt different than my first few combat deployments. I knew the dangers ahead of me, and I was okay with it. I wasn't the wide-eyed, young gunfighter who ached for his first firefight. I saw that in some of my junior men. Professionally, this deployment was at another level. I had to focus on the larger operational and strategic picture. How would my snipers impact company, battalion, and regimental operations. With that, I was no longer a sniper team leader conducting face-to-face missions with my squad leaders. I'd be meeting with Battalion and Regimental commanders. I understood and appreciated the responsibility that came with my position, but I considered it might be more politicking instead of gun fighting.

Excitement ran high sky high with my men. Our warrior culture bred Marines hungry to fight, but those who've experienced combat know that it comes with a price. Some couldn't wait for that first kill or engagement, but killing, death, and all things attached to war changes people. I wasn't worried about my senior Marines who knew what to expect, it was the junior guys that concerned me. Some were in for a rude awakening. I understood how their youthful enthusiasm would eventually give way to a sullen spirit. To me, that was neither good nor bad, just a fact of life for us. Deep down, I truly hoped my men were strong enough to cope with their upcoming experiences.

At Leatherneck, we joined our advanced party, and we were one big happy family again. Our reunion of sorts was short lived. It was the last time we'd all be together until the end of our deployment. Unfortunately, it would be the last time we saw some of our brothers alive. In the time we had, we made last minute preparations and zeroed our weapons. We needed them to be right on target when the fighting started. After finishing our preparations, our Battalion Gunner signed off on our in-country briefs, although we'd never attended a single brief, off we went into the fray.

We flew to FOB (Forward Operating Base) Edinburgh or Edi to those in the Musa Quelah District of Northern Helmand. From there, I sent one team west to the Now Zad District with Lima Company. The rest of my Platoon would support the companies and battalion in Musa Quelah.

We relieved the famous First Battalion Eighth Marines or 1/8 for short. My good friend Jerry commanded their scout/sniper platoon. He had been a fellow Scout/Sniper Instructor and graciously prepared to release his platoon's equipment to us and planned the left seat/right seat missions. Within the first few days, their serialized equipment was ours, and my teams and I were on our first replacement mission.

I joined Reaper Five with Seiple and his team on their missions since I would be with them for the initial part of the deployment. Our first mission was from OP (Observation Post) Panda Ridge, a tiny squad size observation post on the western edge of Battalion's northern area of operations.

There, in our AO (Area of Operations), the enemy held two main strongholds, and they were known to intermingle with the local populace as well. Intelligence reports estimated hundreds of enemy fighters in the wadi to the north, and another couple hundred to the east. Essentially surrounded; that would make finding and killing the enemy much easier. The enemy fighters in the area fell mainly in two groups; Taliban and Insurgents.

The Taliban was Pashtuns, members of Afghan's largest tribe. Most were locals, as well as some Pakistanis.

They called the shots from small unit levels, all the way up to the regional levels.

Insurgents were mostly Taliban recruited locals. They easily blended in as civilians and gained information and access to our infrastructures, but only fought when they had to. Foreign fighters also belonged to the insurgency, their main goal was Jihad and killing infidels. We were more than happy to help all-of-the-above make liaison with Allah and their virgins in the sky.

On March thirteenth, at first light, we headed north up a ridge line on a recon patrol. Reaper Two moved adjacent to us but east and on the opposite ridge. On the way, Reaper Two took heavy machine gun fire. Our team heard the fight and quickly moved to find the enemy, but because of the sparse vegetation in the area, we were exposed and drew enemy fire. Jerry, 1/8's Sniper Platoon Commander, just waved at the enemy and reported the situation. It was a normal day for him.

Within seconds, bullets tilled the earth around us. Luckily, the team on the eastern ridge identified an enemy observer moving along the western side of the wadi. They were out of shooting range and handed us positive identification (PID) to shoot. I acquired the target as he attempted to flee north while tossing his binoculars and radio into the weeds to try and blend in as a farmer. Joey, a seasoned Sergeant and sniper with Reaper Five, sent one round into the man's midsection, dropping him behind a berm 426 meters away. I kept my sights on the immediate area hoping he'd show himself, and wouldn't you know it, my patience paid off. He raised his head to look around; in that split second I centered my crosshairs on his melon and let one fly. The impact of my round hit him in the left eye blowing his brains out the back of his head. It was my very first; a perfect head shot as a sniper. After we knocked him out, the machine gun fire ceased, allowing us to return to OP (Observation Post) Panda Ridge. I couldn't have hoped for a better start to our deployment. It baptized the younger Marines into the art of killing.

The following day, we supported a platoon from India Company, Marines from 1/8, and the ANA (Afghan National Army), on a platoon reinforced sweep of the northern area of our AO. It didn't take long before the platoon was pinned down by intense machine gun fire, but Reaper Two on the east side of the wadi, found and whacked two insurgents from that engagement. Pertaining to enemy causalities, that was the start of Reaper Two's deployment.

The way I saw it, in our AO, squirrel season had arrived, dirt squirrels that is, and the Betio Bastards Sniper Platoon looked to set record bag limits. Within a week, the starting score became three-zero, us, and soon the enemy referred to our platoon as "Ghosts" since we struck from nowhere, and they never found us.
Patrolling Panda Ridge was an experience all its own. The landscape matched America's southwestern high deserts and probably the Moon. There was no vegetation except small patches of short dry grass and small bristled cacti. The

biggest challenge stemmed from the rocky, densely packed soil that perfectly facilitated IED placement.

While we fought up north, Dep and Rob Richards' team, Reaper Four, rocked and rolled down south, beginning to dispatch insurgents. Then Rob, leading a mission with his team, Dep, and combat engineers, incorporated tanks into the fight and set a precedent for the combined use of snipers and tanks for future operations.

It happened when Rob made liaison with a tank platoon commander just a few kilometers away. Reaper Four, Dep, and a combat engineers attachment took a hide site in a building south by southwest of their PB (Patrol Base) Mehraj. This desolate no man's land had become mostly abandoned by civilians due to the rise of insurgent activity. Reaper Four's objective was to find and pick off the insurgents there. The enemy didn't wait long to show themselves, and a group of military-aged males in dark colored dishdashes, typical Taliban fighter garb, gathered nearby. After some observation, the snipers noticed an armed insurgent moving in and out of the compounds. Rob put him down with a single shot from his M40A5.

The team continued watching the area since they were not compromised. They discovered insurgents building a loophole, also known as a murder hole. The enemy used the hole to shoot from and then disappear. The enemy's mistake was aiming the barrel of a weapon toward the patrol base, forcing the team to react. Rob radioed the tank's platoon commander and asked if they wanted to "blow shit up?" "Hell, Yeah," was the response, and the team guided the tanks onto the murder hole. The tanks opened fire with their main guns, killing another bad guy.

At sunset, the team remained vigilant, observing the area and the dead enemy combatants. They understood the possibility of other insurgents moving in to collect their dead. Their perceptiveness paid off. Using thermals, Dep caught four individuals with weapons slung on their backs, low-crawling toward the lifeless bodies. He quickly readied the team, providing the range to targets, while they used night vision to find their targets. Dep marked the targets with a laser. The team fired in unison at each of the individuals. When the shooting stopped, there were four more enemy KIA.

That night, under cover of darkness, the team patrolled back to PB (Patrol Base) Mehraj. The success of that mission and the support of tanks set the platform for larger battalion operations later in the deployment.

About a week later, Reaper Four joined forces with Reaper One at PB 7171. The PB took its name from its geographic location on a map and stood at the southeast corner of our battalion's AO. Pete, our dependable chief scout/sniper and Reaper One's team leader, hailed from New England. His and Rob's teams split up, and a small detachment including the team leaders headed south on a recon patrol, leaving the others behind. They found a prime position with excellent fields of fire and observation to the south. The men called the rest of the teams out and set up an overt position and picked a fight.

Begrudgingly, the rest of the teams packed up their gear, extra water, and chow to meet up with Pete and Rob. They arrived and established shooting positions on the roofs of the compounds to find the enemy. Before long, they spotted two bad guys roughly 850 meters away. Signals intelligence confirmed that the men were discussing our team's location, allowing us to engage them. The men were quickly reduced, adding two more to the tally.

A few hours later, another insurgent carrying a long-barreled AK was caught trying to sneak through a compound. Our group killed him. He unknowingly turned a corner and walked directly into their sights.

The next day, our teams spotted an insurgent using a radio while walking across an area known as the pyramids for its three barren ridge lines sitting east to west south of the PB. He was 1050 meters away, close to the maximum effective range of our rifles, Rob, Pete, Chapps, and Smith fired a coordinated frame shot on the insurgent. A coordinated frame shot is when snipers fire in unison while using slightly varying holds. It's very effective when the target is at a greater distance, and the atmospheric conditions are inconsistent.

After the engagement, the team packed up and patrolled back to PB 7171. Apparently the man on the Icom radio was a very important bad guy and thought to be a High-Value Target. One of the other kills the previous day was a well-known IED maker in the area. Another score for the good guys!

Back up in northern Musa Quelah, in the land of the sun-baked IEDs, Reaper Five and I regularly conducted reconnaissance, ambush, and security patrols along Panda Ridge. During these patrols, we almost always found IEDs or anti-tank mines. It seemed like the IEDs were everywhere. Around the same time, India Company's leadership held a meeting with the local elders at OP Panda Ridge. Josh and I attended the meeting and learned of our impact on insurgents in the area. The elders said that the insurgents feared the "One Shots and Sky People," because every time they went north, their men died. One gentleman said that his brother, who supported the Taliban, had been shot through the left eye in the wadi up north. I smiled inside. We were doing our job.

One memorable ambush patrol was targeting an enemy LP/OP (Listening Post/Observation Post) around the Whiskey sector. A few days prior, we'd missed an 820-meter shot on a bearded insurgent, and we wanted to finish the job. Reaper Five and I sneaked north along the ridge line before the sun came up. Josh, Mattie, Billy A., and I crawled into position. That morning, we caught sight of the bearded observer in an alley. He was behind a wall at 816 meters and exposed his head and neck.

Our four-man element squirmed around in place to keep undiscovered on the barren ridge. After acquiring the target, we adjusted for wind and elevation while Billy focused his spotting scope and counted down for a coordinated shot. Two of our rounds struck the wall just right of the target's head. I found the vapor trail, or trace, from my round as it coursed through the air and dropped down into my field of view in the scope. The round struck the target hitting him in the throat through his long beard. The insurgent twisted and dropped out of sight into the alley. That shot was especially gratifying since we'd missed the same asshole from 850 meters a few days before. Needless to say, we never saw him again.

On another trip along the ridge line with Reaper Five, we found ourselves in a complex ambush. It's funny how our cat and mouse game with insurgents became a normal predicament. Sometimes they found us first, and sometimes we found them first. Our superior marksmanship tended to be the difference, and we hit our marks more often than they did. However, on more than one occasion, we found IEDs and watched bullets splash in the dirt inches from our faces on the ridge.

Reaper Five always performed flawlessly under horrible circumstances. Whether seamlessly controlling supporting arms, rocking out in gunfights or continuously crushing the enemy's attempts to ambush and overwhelm them, they always held their ground. Doc even got some. He is the only man I know with a confirmed kill after blasting an insurgent in the head with a 40mm grenade from an M203 at 150 meters.

Month Two

In April, India Company received intelligence that a JPEL (Joint Prioritized Effects List) target was at an enemy safe house to the north of PB Griffin. It meant all coalition forces in Afghanistan were searching for him. They planned a mission to apprehend the target. The weapons platoon commander traveled to Panda Ridge to give the weapons guys their tasks and to relay the sniper teams' tasks from India Company's commander, Captain Mulvaney. Reaper Five was to be in direct support of India Company for the duration of the operation, along with Reaper Two, already in direct support of India.

Reaper Two was to conduct long-range surveillance on the objective and provide initial terminal guidance (ITG) of the company, along with indicating and providing information on enemy movements. They infiltrated the objective twenty-four hours in advance, climbing Mount Musa Quelah, affectionately known as Mount Doom, the night of the twenty-fifth, to begin reporting back to India Company's Command Post.

By the morning of the twenty-sixth the raid force, (US Marines and ANA) were gathered at PB Griffin on the east side of the wadi. Reaper Five and I, a squad from weapons, and their Lieutenant sat ready to go on the west side.

The weapons squad established a support by fire position on the west side of the wadi in order to interdict enemy reinforcements moving to the east. Reaper Five moved farther north along the western side of the wadi. They'd be clearing a route for the weapons squad, marking the support by fire (SBF) position, and providing indications and warnings of enemy movements. If successful they would be reducing selected targets and targets of opportunity.

We departed friendly lines around 2200 and began sweeping a route north along Panda Ridge. We marked every possible IED we ran across in order to warn the weapons guys behind us. We also informed the weapons platoon leaders to make sure to stay away from the crest of the ridge line and keep west of the old Russian trench systems.

By 0100 on the twenty-seventh, we'd moved approximately two kilometers north of OP Panda Ridge and were about a kilometer and a half from our hide site. Silently we moved north until a loud explosion captured our attention. It originated from our south about 800 meters away. I happened to be looking in that direction and witnessed a flash from the explosion in my NODs (night optical devices). I knew right away what happened, and immediately felt anger fill the pit of my stomach. One of the Marines from weapons had struck an IED.

Pandemonium ensued as the men worked to save the Marine while calling in a medevac, but nothing could be done to save him. We pushed out and set up a security perimeter to monitor the likely enemy avenues of approach from the north and the east. Once the dust off medevac came in for the Marine, we moved back south and linked up with the weapons Marines to provide security while we waited for sunrise and EOD.

At sunrise, Josh, a few senior Marines, and I helped the Lieutenant and his Marines search for pieces of the Marine and his kit. We couldn't find everything and assumed it was destroyed by the blast, but another Marine did find one more IED. Unfortunately, we couldn't search into the wadi because of the high IED threat and the fact that we would be outnumbered five to one.

Around mid-morning, EOD met us, and we needed a guide to link up with them. Two Marines from Reaper Five and I headed west for the task. After taking EOD to the blast site, they found another IED, putting a total of three in a twenty-meter radius. The EOD guys said the IED had been there for approximately a month, maybe two. Ironically about a week prior, I'd walked all over that area with Josh while using part of the old trench for a hide site/OP. I'd taken a shit a couple feet from the IED that hit the Marine. I realized how easily Josh or I could have bought the big one ourselves. Once the EOD techs set the charges on the IEDs and completed their post-blast analysis, we moved to cover, allowing the techs to blow the IEDs. Reaper Five and I then led the weapons guys out of the area back to OP Panda Ridge.

We arrived at Panda Ridge and talked to the Marine's Platoon Sergeant, Sergeant Penny, who explained he hadn't survived his injuries and had died on the way to FOB Edi. I broke the bad news to Josh and his team while Doc helped medevac a Marine named Carr, from weapons. He was starting to show severe traumatic brain injury (TBI) symptoms and had to go.

Shortly after the mission, we learned that the target house was a dry hole, just as the guys from Reaper Two had warned. Days later, India Company's Commander restricted our movement to the north on Panda Ridge, and at the Operation Officer's request, I moved Reaper Five to Deh Karez on our eastern AO boundary.

At Deh Karez, we met a hard charging infantry platoon with weapons attachments and an awesome Platoon Commander named Joe. He solely wanted to fuck up the Taliban. There was also a small contingent of ANP (Afghan National Police) and surprisingly, they were very proficient.

Their patrol base desperately needed sniper support. Just like most of the positions in the AO, ground forces had minimal freedom of movement due to the enemy's extensive observation networks, directly linked to a linear defense-in-depth in most areas. I made it a priority to explain to all five of my teammates to concentrate on this network for the first month, in order to defeat the enemy's lines of communication. In doing so, we gouged the enemy's eyes and forced them to be more reactive.

Just outside and surrounding Deh Karez, a small group of ridge lines took shape around 900-1700 meters from the base. The enemy loved to observe the infantry squad's movements from that area, but the Marines, although knowingly being observed, couldn't engage the enemy because of a nearby village that would have taken collateral damage. For that reason, the area was tailor-made for my snipers.

Reaper Five and I arrived late in the night to Deh Karez, allowing us to conceal our sniper rifles, especially from the ANP (Afghan National Police). We weren't quite positive that they were all on our side. For days, we watched the surrounding areas until noticing an active observer and machine gun team on a ridge to the northeast about 1,000 meters out. They appeared every evening and were fully aware that the Marines on the post wouldn't fire on them. That's where we stepped in.

By the third day, the observers appeared as usual, but we were ready for them. A sniper named Mattie occupied post one with his M40, and I took a position at a loophole in the wall I'd made facing the ridge line. I also had my M40. Completely exposed to Mattie and me at 975 meters away, the three insurgents were about to get a big surprise. Josh counted down, and we fired a beautifully executed coordinated shot knocking two insurgents back over the ridge line as they held their torsos. I put a follow-up shot for good measure. I realized afterward I didn't have time to get properly dressed. It was the first time I'd killed a man while wearing nothing but shorts and flip-flops. Killing the enemy seemed more important than looking proper at the time.

We sent a squad of ANP to recover the enemy bodies and equipment. When they returned, they reported puddles of blood on the ground, and they'd witnessed two motorcycles dragging away two bodies.

The engagement forced insurgents to assume more distant positions. One was a ridge 1,400 meters to our east. I guess they figured they'd be out of our range, allowing them to continue observing our patrols.

What they didn't know, we had the M107 Barrett .50 caliber Special Application Scoped Rifle (SASR). While not technically a sniper rifle, the SASR was devastating in the right hands. Joey, one of my snipers from Reaper Five, proved to have the right hands, whacking an insurgent in the new enemy observation post, a 1400 meter hit.

8 MID-DEPLOYMENT

Month Three

I assisted Reaper Five at Deh Karez for a few weeks in May,
killing more dirt squirrels and visiting Reaper Two at Griffin
from time to time. All my teams were shining when I
returned to the Battalion Command Post for my monthly
synchronization meeting and serialized gear inventory. By
then it was mid-May, and my platoon sat at seventy-five
confirmed kills, a handful of possibles, and quite a few
supporting arms kills. The command couldn't have been
more pleased with our work and results.

I learned that our battalion planned to establish a
patrol base in the southern Now Zad district at Salaam

Bazaar. Salaam Bazaar was notorious for its illicit market, ripe with arms and drugs, as well as being a key logistics hub for the Taliban. Large amounts of drugs, weapons, and cash funneled through the market to the Musa Quelah and Sangin areas. Our battalion aimed to curb the traffic by sticking Marines right on the X.

The Taliban and their insurgent friends the that we were building a patrol base in their back yard. The construction of the PB was a joint effort between Lima and Kilo Companies, with Kilo clearing the area and Lima holding the patrol base to conduct operations.

On May 15th, before the patrol base was complete, and after Kilo Company had withdrawn, the PB was attacked. Reaper One and Three were in direct support of the defense and found themselves in the middle of the mayhem. It started after the departure of Kilo. The insurgents waited and initiated contact on the Salaam Bazaar PB with an 84mm recoilless rifle and medium machine guns. Marines in the main PB reacted quickly. A small contingent, a platoon from Lima Company, their command element, and Sniper Teams One and Three, were on their own at the southernmost battle position of the AO. The first barrage hit one of my snipers, Andrew, severely injuring his left leg. Fortunately our Corpsman, Doc Devin, was nearby and acted fast with help from two other Marines, they quickly patched him up.

Under fire, Chris rolled underneath a truck shouting his leg hurt. He had a chunk of shrapnel, and so did Reaper

One's team leader, Pete, who had burning metal in his legs and back. Despite his wounds, Pete helped Chris move to the medevac site as the firefight heated up. Amid the fierce barrage, Jerome and Clay from Reaper One took positions atop the dirt-filled Hesco barriers engaging targets despite being completely exposed to enemy fire. They were both wounded as a result but continued to fight. Clay methodically took out targets, as Doc Devin worked on Jerome and helped to evacuate him and Pete on the second bird, all while AGS-17 and heavy machine gun fire landed around them.

Later, multiple witnesses said that my Marines responded to the attack by covering each other and continually seeking positions to engage the enemy. They fought like true warriors during the chaos and responded flawlessly to the enemy while caring for their brothers. Doc Devin, Clay, Pete, and the Company First Sergeant were awarded Bronze Stars with devices for Valor for their actions that day. Ross and Jerome were awarded the Navy and Marine Corps Commendation Medals with Valor for actions in combat as well. What an honor to have served with such a group of heroes!

When I caught wind of the attack and realized that my Marines got hurt, I made my way down to Salaam Bazaar. I sent Deptula to Deh Karez with Reaper Five. I was furious Battalion took two days to get word to me of the injuries. I also learned my Marines, though wounded, had tried to refuse medical attention. Clay denied the medevac;

Pete returned after threatening to jump out of the chopper, and Andrew, Chris, and Jerome flew to Bastian and Leatherneck. Their injuries required them to leave the country. Chris refused to leave while Andrew and Jerome had no choice.

I arrived at Salaam Bazaar on the afternoon of the 19th. The remaining members of Reaper One and Three were on an ambush mission east of the Bazaar. The next morning around 0600, they caught six insurgents during a meeting. The beautiful thing, the bad guys, were only eighty-seven yards from their hide. My snipers made them pay for their stupidity. The sight of my guys returning with an M105 trailer full of enemy corpses was amazing. I knew right then they were going to be okay. They were even tougher and more resilient than I had anticipated. Good thing they were so tenacious because they'd need every ounce of determination and strength in the coming months.

Just as every place Marines occupy, the living conditions were horrid at Salaam Bazaar. Our patrol base was a 100-meter by 100-meter triangle at the edge of a dry wadi full of fine talcum powder dust. The summer months ushered in the 120 days of wind, as one can imagine; the dust and sand took on lives of their own. It consumed everything and to add to the misery, the heat rose to unbelievable temperatures, routinely upwards of 130° F. We did have two 10x12 cooling tents with AC units, but they worked only intermittently.

The base sat 1500 meters from the actual bazaar and believe me, every bit of open field and sandy shit shacks between us became contested ground. At first, the Marines couldn't push past more than a few hundred meters without making enemy contact. The boot ass Lieutenant from Lima Company kept sending his men into ambushes by continually forcing them on contact patrols with no tactical advantage or purpose. As snipers, we used the predictability of the enemy's reaction to the squads to our advantage.

Before long, we had an 800-meter buffer around the patrol base, allowing the squads freedom of movement. But instead of taking advantage of the buffer created by my snipers, the Lieutenant, instead, pushed his patrols farther outside the bubble. He ignored the advice of the locals. A big mistake. He wasn't even trying to build a reputation with the local leaders. Instead, he was chasing ghosts and medals across open fields swept with machine gun fire. What a fucking moron.

During one of these contact patrols, Reaper Three thrust our unit into the international spotlight. They destroyed an enemy machine gun team with two 250-pound JDAMs (Joint Direct Attack Munitions) and accidentally killed civilians in the process. While an unfortunate mistake, it was the only thing that could have been done to save the Marines on the ground. Tragically, the civilians had been hidden out of sight.

Reaper Three set out on a mission on the night of May 27th and settled into a hide south of the PB but north of the

Bazaar. They had perfect sights on known enemy positions and ingress and egress routes. A squad planned to patrol the area between Reaper Three and the PB. Instead, the patrol leader took his Marines across an open field heading straight toward the enemy stronghold at the Bazaar. Once in the middle of the field, the insurgents let loose, pinning the Marines down in the open field. Dog handler Lance Corporal Peter Clore was hit immediately and lay severely bleeding from his wounds.

Reaper Three began prosecuting targets and requesting air support to engage a four-man machine gun team. Cheese, the JTAC (Joint Terminal Attack Controller) attached to Weapons Company, sent the transmission. Once approved, minutes later two JDAMs decimated the compound used by insurgents.

The bombs repelled the attack, but it was too late for Clore. The men around him couldn't save him, the sheer volume of enemy fire prevented them from moving. He and a wounded local national were transported by QRF vehicles for medevac. When things calmed a bit, a post-blast analysis determined that the insurgents weren't the only people occupying the compound. A family was also inside. Eight women and children died as a result of the bombing. The Battalion's civil affairs detachment provided supplies paid the family for their damage and their dead. War truly is hell.

While I helped Reaper One and Three down south, up north, it appeared Reaper Two enjoyed a little payback of their own. They left on a planned hunting mission north of

PB Griffin, the Battalion's northern-most position located opposite the wadi east of OP Panda Ridge. The team departed before dawn, using the elevated ridge lines to conceal their movement from the enemy in the valley below. Staying just below the crest, they stepped only on the hard rock to avoid the ever-present IEDs that laced the footpaths. At that elevation, they were able to pick out the freshly planted IEDs on the trails below.

The Marines moved undetected roughly two kilometers north of Griffin and set up their position. Established, with security in place, Nate, Mac, and Mark observed west into the valley. The farmers there openly supported the Taliban, allowing them to use their compounds and fields for lookouts and firing positions. The team knew it would be a matter of time until they caught the enemy.

Soon Nate noticed something suspicious. It was a spotter. He was in the village crouched in the corner of a graveyard and talking on an Icom radio while observing the infantry patrolling through the valley's green zone. Adam, the team's signal intelligence attachment, picked up the conversation, listened for twenty minutes before eagerly explaining the spotter was reporting information to a High-Value Target named Mr. Dirkha. He's equivalent to a Platoon Sergeant, which meant his responsibility was coordinating attacks on coalition patrols and patrol bases.

While Adam explained what he'd learned, the spotter they were watching walked down the hill toward a tree line the insurgents frequently used to shoot. The snipers tracked his every move while discussing whether or not to shoot. They considered the extreme range, in excess of 1000 meters and missed their opportunity when the spotter disappeared into the trees. Disheartened by second-guessing themselves, the team received good news from Adam.

The spotter planned to meet with Mr. Dirkha and walk to his house! Twenty seconds later he appeared again and marched directly toward the team's position. As he approached the middle of the wadi, a second man stepped from a house directly below the snipers. Adam's face shined with excitement. He believed the man walking toward the spotter was Mr. Dirkha. Nate, the team leader, made the decision to wait until the two met before engaging.

The team readied their weapons while the two targets casually neared each other. Once the two were face-to-face and shook hands, the team ranged them at 736 meters. Just as the spotter bowed to the other man, the snipers opened fire in unison - Nate on the M40, Mark on theM110, Mac on the M107 SASR, and Grayson with the M240B machine gun. The wall of lead dropped both targets, killing the spotter and severely wounding the other who tried crawling. Mac wasn't about to let that filthy animal get away and fired the M107. Nate and Mark witnessed the explosive Raufus rounds spark on the rock underneath the insurgent's body. Grayson sent a few well-aimed bursts from the machine gun for good measure to ensure he stayed down for good.

Following the engagement, Mr. Dirkha screamed over the radio, "The Americans killed two more of my men. My Bodyguard and Senior Spotter!" It seemed the plan was the Bodyguard was to escort the Spotter to Mr. Dirkha's location. The team had mistaken the bodyguard for the HVT.

From their position, the team had eyes on both dead fighters. They decided to remain in place to interdict possible enemy activity and reported the situation to the COC, Combat Operations Center. An hour passed; it became apparent the insurgents were through playing for the day. The team picked up and navigated the ridge lines back toward the base. Along the way, Adam overheard a brief argument between Mr. Dirkha and the senior Taliban commander in Northern Helmand, Mr. Khar.

"Gather your fighters, go into the mountains, and kill the Sky People!" commanded Mr. Khar. Sky People referred to the snipers at Griffin.

"If you want them, you go after them yourself!" barked Mr. Dirkha.

It was obvious we were devastating the Taliban in the north. We were killing not just the fighters but also their Commanders. That level of insubordination was unheard of within the Taliban. The enemy was scared and lived in constant fear both day and night, that's just what we wanted.

About a week after this patrol, Nate and his team had another mission to interdict enemy forces to the north. Nate was awakened in the early hours by Adam excitedly explaining that approximately 30 new fighters were on their way to join the fight in and around PB Griffin. Nate ran down to the COC and got on the radio with the India Company Commander, Captain M. He explained the situation and received permission to go out and set an ambush on the advancing fighters.

Nate quickly readied his team; they were soon geared up ready to go. They patrolled north, using the ridge lines as cover, to an area about four kilometers away overlooking known enemy positions. They patrolled past the no man's land of abandoned buildings and fields and skirted around the enemy's observation post and spotters into their back yard. They set up a position at the north edge of no man's land. Once in position they watched and waited for the enemy to show themselves.

At first light, the insurgents showed their hand when they launched two recoilless rifle rounds at PB Griffin, hitting just south of the patrol base's observation post. The enemy then moved along the west side of the wadi in the trees. Nate picked up their movement and saw the individual with the rocket on his back along with five other insurgents. Nate and Smith opened up on them with the M40A5 and M240, initiating what would turn out to be a very long day. Their initial volley killed two insurgents immediately and possibly two more that they weren't able to confirm by visual means.

Nate and his team then realized they had a large contingent of insurgents in fixed positions in the compounds just 300 meters north of the tree line. The Marines at PB Griffin readied three squads to move out and push north and get into the fight. The insurgents could be heard over the radio in a total panic trying to maneuver their men into position to attack the Marines coming out of the patrol base and evacuate their leadership.

Nate got on the M107 SASR and began engaging the insurgents as they tried leaving the compound 1400 meters away. He laid down three to five round bursts as individuals tried exiting the compound. He wanted to hold them in place for the advancing infantry platoon. Nate held them for about an hour as the infantry pushed north.

Once the Marines in the green zone reached the west side of the wadi, the insurgents opened up on the infantrymen with Dshk .51 caliber machine guns. They fired from two positions to the north, from the tree line on the eastern side of the wadi. From the information gathered by signals intelligence, the Taliban was attempting to delay our ground troops from the south until their leadership could evacuate the area.

Nate moved Mark to the SASR and began relaying information to higher ups while trying to spot enemy movement in the valley. Mark located an insurgent in the area of the compounds maneuvering at about 1500 meters and dropped him in his tracks with a .50 caliber round from the SASR.

As the snipers engaged the insurgents to the far north, the infantry began to move up the wadi. They were soon pinned down by the Dshk fire. Recoilless rifle rounds wounded Marines with shrapnel. With the Platoon Commander, one of the Squad Leaders, and another Marine hurt, they needed help quickly. CAAT moved up from the PB as a mounted QRF to support the infantry fighting on the ground. The wounded needed evacuation. It was too hot to get air evac to help. As CAAT moved up the Wadi, one of their vehicles got stuck in the river, the rest pushed towards the Marines position. The vehicles came under fire from the Dshk machine guns. They called in fixed wing air support. Once the birds were on station things got loud. Jets swooped out of the sky dropping two 500 pound bombs on the enemy compound.

Nate and his team relocated to the north of their original position to get a better vantage point on the enemy and provide support for the Marines pinned down. Pinpointing the location of the Dshk machine gun was a must. As Nate rounded a corner of the terrain, he saw a mass of IED material. Battery packs and pressure plates. There weren't any main charges, so he scooped up the battery packs and pressure plate switches and kept moving north looking for a better vantage point. Once in position, they located one of the Dshk machine guns, reported the position and a jet put a 500 pounder on it, silencing the enemy position.

From their new position, to get eyes on the enemy, the Marine snipers had to expose themselves and their position. The dirt kicked up around them, as the enemy tried to silence their mortal enemy in the hills. The snipers laid down suppressive fire and broke contact, in search of a more concealed place to engage the enemy.

Once in position on a small rise on the ridge line, Nate spotted the enemy in the tree line to the north along the east side of the wadi. He once again directed air on the enemy position. They dropped another 500 pounder on the assholes and their other Dshk. After the bombing, Nate spotted four insurgents trying to put IEDs into the wadi north of CAATs position. Two of the dirt squirrels were digging holes, and the other two were following in trace laying in the HME IEDs. They'd obviously done it before, they were putting the IEDs in within a matter of minutes.

With the machine guns silenced, Cobras came on station and immediately started in on the insurgents. Their first pass churned up dirt along both sides of the insurgents setting the IEDs. All four began running. The choppers came back around and hit two of the insurgents with a Hellfire missile, blowing them to pieces. Then the Cobra's Dash Two came in behind, mopping up the other two with his coaxial machine guns.

After about ten hours of carnage, the insurgents were done playing and were running out of light. Just like cockroaches, they scurried back into their holes and began to disappear. Once the battlefield settled, the Marines began the slow patrol moving back south to their PB. Both the Battalion and Company Commands were extremely happy with the results of Reaper Two. They'd provided significant help to their brother Marines on the ground.

Towards the end of May, after the airstrike and Clore's death down south, we continued to take the fight to the enemy. We hoped to focus solely on the enemy's continued defense of Salaam Bazaar and their repetitive use of the same well-established fighting positions. By then, Weapons Company had taken control of PB Salaam Bazaar from Lima and PB Shir Ghazy from Kilo in the east. It meant a change of command. A young, recently promoted Captain replaced the Lieutenant. He seemed to have a solid grasp on reality and the situation at the Bazaar. Unfortunately, it also meant sending Reaper Three to Now Zad with Lima Company. Our sniper presence dwindled to Reaper One, some engineers, and me at Salaam Bazaar. Because of casualties, I rotated a few guys around the teams to even them out. After that, we ran missions providing watch for the squads, sometimes using them as bait, particularly the 81mm mortar platoon. On one mission, the 'bait' technique worked amazingly well.

We moved under the cover of darkness to a compound 500 meters from the center of the Bazaar and waited on the sun to rise. At around 0600, the squad from 81s, along with the Captain, was on the move, headed in our direction. We waited patiently to spring the trap, and it didn't take long until insurgents attempted to maneuver against the squad.

Pete and Jerry struck first, engaging two insurgents to the north. Shortly afterward, Cobb killed an insurgent to the east, and Brett engaged with the M240 machine gun. I saw a Spotter above the market on the roof of a building 600 meters away. The wind blew gently from my back directly toward the target. It was perfect and would have no effect on my bullet. I settled my crosshairs directly on his head and shoulders and squeezed off a shot. Put one right through the insurgent's face, knocking him off the roof.

Cobb shot another insurgent to the east, and I gut shot an asshole creeping in the market with an AK47. We continued back and forth for nearly an hour. The squad killed a few insurgents in a tree line, and things quieted down as QRF (Quick React Force) came to pull us out.

The gateways in and out of compounds were frequently laced with IEDs and were ideal targeting areas for enemy snipers. Our engineers blew a hole in the compound wall for us to exit through. We jumped on the trucks without taking enemy fire, then headed back to PB Salaam Bazaar. Score one for the good guys. The mission gave the 81s, normally strictly mortar men who turned into a line platoon, a lot more breathing room.

9 OUR LOSS

Month Four

On June 2, I traveled to Weapons Company's CP (Command Post) at Shir Ghazy. The trip was to discuss scout/sniper employment with Captains Alsop and McCoy, two of the best Officers I've worked with. I anticipated a quick trip before heading back to Salaam Bazaar once we'd finished planning future missions. The night before leaving, I sat in the COC with First Sergeant Combs and Master Sergeant Long, when India Company to the north called in a Medevac. The ZAP number passed over the net was MAB8882. The number stood for a Marine's first initial, last initial, blood type, and last four of their social security. Hearing the numbers was like taking a punch in the gut.

I instantly recognized it as Sergeant Mark A. Bradley,

one of my snipers and the Assistant Team Leader for Reaper Two. I took a knee in the COC (Command Operations Center) and listened to the radio traffic. Mark was being medically evacuated after stepping on a pressure plate IED.

I was angry and heartbroken. I couldn't believe another one of my Marines took a hit, but Mark was strong and would fight for his life. He had a warrior's spirit and was taking the fight to the enemy before being wounded. Losing such a good sniper, Marine, and brother in the platoon was a heavy blow.

As hard as it was for the rest of us in the platoon, it was a life-changing event for the men of Reaper Two. We learned when Mark stepped on the IED, their mission called for them to interdict the enemy, whose presence had increased with the start of summer, their fighting season. The team operated nearly every day, constantly maintaining contact with the enemy, and regularly killing them.

They planned to infiltrate under darkness deep into enemy territory that early morning to observe a known insurgent meeting location. That evening, the team finished last minute preparations and bedded down for a rest before departing friendly lines. Mac double checked his M4 and inserted a full mag with a round in the chamber. His biggest fear was one of the ANA, or ANP would have a change of heart and kill the Marines in their sleep. It happened before, plus the local ANA and ANP had already been caught communicating with insurgents, informing them over the radio of the Marines' locations. That's why Mac slept with a loaded gun.

Suddenly, while they were sleeping, a large explosion shook the team from their racks. Nate, Mac, Mark, Creep, and another sniper in the team ran to the COC for answers. The huge explosion originated exactly where the team planned to move in the morning. They hoped it was some dumb ass Taliban fighters blowing themselves up while emplacing an IED, but there was no way of knowing until morning.

The sun slowly broke over the horizon on the eastern side of Mt. Doom when Reaper Two sneaked into position. They would be overlooking one of the most heavily saturated Taliban villages in the area. Because of the explosion the night before, they moved slowly and cautiously entering their hide site. On the move, they found a fresh crater furrowed into the earth. Thirty feet away they saw the mangled remains of a dog. The insurgents had placed an IED on the footpath in hopes that the snipers would step on it. Unfortunately, their emplacement skills had grown and had the dog not activated the IED, one or more in the team would've been blown to bits. The men continued slowly moving up the hill, after twenty minutes, they decided to turn back. While moving back, Mark found an IED just two feet away from Mac, saving his brother from a painful death.

Back at PB Griffin, the team removed their gear. Tension filled the air, and an unsettling feeling sat inside all of them. They realized that they'd become specific targets to insurgents, who began saturating every footpath they believed the snipers would use with IEDs. The team's next step was to develop a plan to counter the bombs, and they immediately began a map study to do so. They decided against moving along the ridge lines unless accompanied by EOD (Explosive Ordinance Disposal) support. They'd blow every IED they found, in place, even using dummy charges to trick the enemy into thinking the Marines were finding more than they did. After the explosions, they'd hold up nearby and ambush the insurgents who returned to check on their handy work.

Shortly afterward, the team set out to set an ambush the enemy as the sun dipped below the horizon. They planned to set off dummy charges where they'd previously found IEDs to render safe the possible IEDs they'd found a few days earlier. They dropped infrared chemical lights on their way, marking a route from the PB for the EOD Marines behind them. The EOD Marines destroyed IEDs and sat off dummy charges as planned. This time our snipers hunted in two elements, Alpha, and Bravo, with Mark's team sitting on a hill facing the IED hot spot to the south. If the Taliban scum wanted to play, Mark and his men were in position, waiting. The other element, with Nate and Mac, began pushing farther north with EOD to an area overlooking the Wadi, an area full of frequent enemy activity.

After being in position for about an hour, Mark called Mac on the radio reporting he saw very dim lights moving through the hills in the distance. Nate and Mac immediately displaced their element and moved to Mark's location. By then, the insurgents had slipped over a small hill and out of sight. The team decided to try and maneuver on them. Mark pointed where he wanted to move, and Nate's element took the lead, pushing forward on the hardened rocks below the horizon, staying out of the enemy's view. Mark's team trailed, and when the snipers were one hundred meters from the hill, an unforgettable explosion unlike any they'd heard before ripped through the bones of Reaper Two.

The blast instantly crippled everyone's hearing, and the shock wave sent a few Marines into vertigo. The damage only meant one thing: Corpsman up! "That was a God damned IED!" Mac screamed to Nate. It was a moment the Marines dreaded. "Turn on a white light! Somebody turn on a fucking white light!" screamed Mac. He knew the IEDs were victim operated, meaning someone stepped on a pressure plate detonating a main charge buried under the earth. As Nate and Mac ran to the back of the patrol, a single white light sparkled. "Who is it? Who the fuck's hit?" Mac heard Grayson's voice speak up, "It's Mark man. It's fucking Mark." The Team Leaders commanded everyone to hold position fearing the possibility of secondary bombs. Experience taught where there's one; there's probably two or more.

As Nate and Mac found Mark, Grayson and Doc already applied tourniquets above his knees. Both his legs were blown off. Brendan, the team's RTO (Radio Operator) and a solid infantry NCO, called a CasEvac (Causality Evacuation) as the Marines tried desperately to help their fallen brother. Mac ran a secondary blood sweep around Mark's head searching for other injuries. He also had a broken arm. Grayson wrapped the arm while Doc applied an IV to feed fluids into his broken body. Mac tilted Mark's head back to keep his airway open, and when he put his hands on Mark's face, the wounded warrior opened his eyes. His brothers spoke to him and tried talking to keep him conscious as long as possible, but Mark couldn't talk. The only way they knew he could hear them was when he blinked his eyes when Mac asked him to do so. Soon afterward, he did begin talking, asking what happened and what was going on.

In the midst of the chaos, the radio crackled, "Reaper Two, be advised there appear to be twelve to fifteen lights moving in a Ranger file toward your location from the north." The news took things from really bad to holy fucking shit. Mac looked to Grayson, "Well this is gonna suck." Mac and Nate yelled to the security element to hold in place and kill any and everyone who approached the team. The Marines turned off all lights except one single light on Mark and waited. They prayed the rescue bird would hurry the fuck up.

In the distance, the team heard rotors approaching from the inbound Dust Off. Dust Off was the call sign for the Medevac Blackhawks from FOB Edi. As the bird approached, Mac, Nate, Grayson, and Doc rolled Mark onto the litter, picked him up as the bird touched down in the designated LZ. Everyone gritted their teeth and walked as fast as possible, fully expecting to step on another IED. Once Mark was on the bird, they said their goodbyes and watched it fly off with their brother. On the ground, the team collected all of the scattered gear and covered the blood, not wanting to give the Taliban the satisfaction of knowing that they had injured a Marine.

The team quickly made it to PG Griffin without incident and handed over all Mark's serialized gear to the Commander. They silently sat outside the tent. Some smoked; others simply gazed into the night sky still covered in their brother's blood. Reality hit hard. War was suddenly very real. You can kill one hundred of them, but you will never fully know the reality of war until you see firsthand one of your brothers wounded or killed.

That night, we all waited anxiously for word concerning Mark's condition. The following day Reaper Two traveled to the battalion's command post for a break. Mark was a fighter, and the last information received stated he was in stable condition at Leatherneck, waiting for transport to Germany.

Down south, I had an immediate problem. Mark's Brother Steven, also a sniper in my platoon with Reaper Four, needed to escort his brother home. I sent word to PB Mehraj and the Battalion Commander. He reacted quickly and got Steven on a bird so he could accompany his brother to Germany, and eventually to the Naval Hospital in Bethesda, Maryland.

The bad news piled up. Shortly after Mark's incident, a Marine in Reaper Three, Aaron, learned that his brother, a Marine with Third Battalion, Fourth Marines was killed in Sangin. Aaron was evacuated from Lima's AO to escort his brother's body back to their father in California.

I reevaluated the teams, once more making personnel changes since six of my men had now been evacuated. The Marines understood war and were extremely tough and resilient. Since he was closer in distance, Dep, the Platoon Sergeant, immediately joined Reaper Two. He started the deployment with Reaper Four at Merhaj but had been at 7171 with Reaper Five when Mark evacuated.

Around the same time, two of my teams, Reaper Four, and Five ran a company level sniper operation east of 7171. It was on the Battalion and Kilo's southeastern boundaries. The disruption operation targeted an enemy stronghold and logistics routes in a village called Say Chow. The significance of the mission was two-fold. First, snipers were the main effort, a strategy the unit hadn't done before, and second, it was one of the first missions of this scale incorporating tanks in direct support of snipers.

The Marines inserted at night and patrolled three kilometers. Tanks staged at PB 7171 and awaited the team's call. Early the next morning, the reinforced sniper teams began engaging targets in a two-story building. The insurgents, oblivious to the sniper's location, huddled together in an alley between two buildings, a big mistake. The team had a line of sight on the targets and unloaded with their sniper rifles and machine guns. The insurgents didn't have a chance; most fell in the immediate barrage. The wounded tried to escape but were mowed down like grass. The tanks moved in as reinforcements to trap the enemy in the kill zone. The plan worked perfectly, and the combined forces systematically picked off insurgents for hours. That day the snipers killed nine insurgents, and the tanks got almost a dozen more.

When I heard about the mission, I was very excited and proud of my Marines for their success. Despite all of our platoon's casualties, they were still unafraid to take the fight to the enemy. During the Say Chow operation, I made a trip to the Battalion Command Post at the Musa Quelah District Center. The Battalion Staff, especially the Operations Officer, praised my men and the tankers for what they'd accomplished for Kilo Company. After my business was through, I traveled back to Salaam Bazaar.

At Salaam Bazaar, I was summoned to the COC. Captain Alsop, our Company Commander, was on the phone. He explained, with a voice filled with sorrow and pain, at 0120 Eastern Standard Time, on 16 June 2012; Sergeant Mark Andrew Bradley succumbed to his wounds. He passed away Surrounded by his family and fellow snipers who arrived to show support.

The news of Mark's passing was devastating. I felt like a knife was being twisted in the pit of my stomach. I'd lost buddies before, quite a few, and it never got easier. I tried numbing it. It was the first time I'd lost a Marine directly under my charge. He wasn't just one of my Marines; he was a friend, fellow scout/sniper, a husband, son, and brother. I'd deployed with him to Iraq with 2/8 in 2006, and I wanted to make these bastards pay for taking such a good Marine and man from us.

The next morning Reaper One and I went hunting Taliban, who made it all too easy. An asshole about 500 meters from the Post continually organized meetings to coordinate insurgent movement and direct enemy activity in the area with his Icom radio. With good observation techniques and a little help from Signals Intelligence, we were able to gain PID (Positive Identification) and hostile intent. Inside Post One, we tracked his movement and only engaged when he was clear of civilians, but our first volley missed. Our lead was a little off; we missed our Mover! We fired in full value fifteen mile per hour winds. Thank God Almighty for suppressors, he didn't hear us. He came right back out from behind the compound where he'd ducked. He was confused as to where the shots originated. This time we were ready. Jerry and I drilled him in the chest with a coordinated shot. As luck would have it, I was in shorts and flip-flops once again.

Not long afterward, our Platoon, minus part of Reaper Three, traveled to the district center of Musa Quelah for Mark's Memorial Service. The mood was very solemn yet filled with purpose. We all wanted to honor Mark the best way we could, and we all wanted to get back to work and make these assholes pay. It was hard to grieve in the middle of a war. We did not have the luxury of time or the ability to 'take a break.' The enemy didn't care, and the war didn't stop. It was, however, nice to see my team together, but not at the cost of a Memorial Service for our brother.

Mark was a constant source of experience in the platoon. He was an exemplary Marine, dedicated scout/sniper, and an older brother to all in the platoon. I'm honored to have served with such a man. For me, writing letters to Mark's family and speaking at his Memorial Service were without a doubt the hardest things I've ever done. Words cannot express the pain a Marine feels when he loses one of his brothers. My heart goes out to his family and friends and to anyone who has experienced such loss.

When we started operations again, our men were aching to fight. Needless to say, our kill count continued to climb, and by the first of July, we had over 150 confirmed kills and still climbing. If we kept up that pace, we would indeed be the most effective scout/sniper platoon since Vietnam.

10 HEATING UP

Deh Karez

Up north, Nate and Reaper Two successfully hunted Taliban
fighters, cutting them down at an impressive rate. Shortly
after Mark's memorial, their first task arose. Marines at Deh
Karez took fire every time they departed base. One Marine
was shot, and another stepped on an IED. Artillery killed a
few enemy fighters but didn't stop them from providing
daily harassment. Reaper Two was ordered to interdict the
enemy network and stop the attacks.

The team moved bases and arrived with Nate
marching directly to the COC (Command Operations
Center) for information while the team settled in. Mac
vocalized what they all knew: Deh Karez was one of the
nastiest areas around. If the Helmand Province was the

ghetto of Afghanistan, then Deh Karez was the ghetto inside the ghetto. The Marines dubbed the area the 'Wild West' because we were told to expect a fight every time we departed the base.

Nate talked with the Platoon Sergeant, Platoon Commander, and the Company Executive Officer. They explained to Nate the Taliban's movements, their preference for traveling in the mornings and hiding a few kilometers north. Once there, Observers scoured the Patrol Base for departing Marines then alerted their fighters and leaders to the Marine activity. They even pointed out the enemy's preferred machine gun locations. Surprisingly, the company was so desperate they planned a mission that would send their patrols out as bait, waiting to get ambushed so Nate's team could flank the enemy and take them out. To Nate, that wasn't an option. He sought out and talked to the Intel rep, who revealed the enemy's meeting places, primarily a mosque, sleep areas, and identified local leadership. He also learned that fighters funneled down the Wadi from the north.

After careful consideration, Nate formulated a plan. Instead of risking lives unnecessarily in a counter-ambush, he decided to attack the source of the problem despite the risk. His team needed to infiltrate a compound on a small hill close to the mosque, which would provide views of the entire area. No units had moved that close to the enemy there. A CAAT section that had been running patrols near the area would insert them and extract them nearly forty-eight hours later. Nate reiterated planning for the heat. It played a major factor. Daylight Temperatures soared upwards of 130°F. The solution was for everyone to fill their packs with at least thirty bottles of water, plus two additional sea bags of water for the mission.

Since it was their first operation after Mark's death, and it being so fresh on the team's mind, they wanted nothing more than a good fight. Their stored aggression showed on their young faces. Because this was a new AO, and Mark succumbed to an IED, some Marines were apprehensive. It was a bold plan. Mark's death revealed how susceptible we were to IEDs. That very scary thought became very real, and Nate needed to find a way to push some of his men past their fears. The easy thing to do would be to settle on the counter-ambush mission, which was relatively safe. Punch out a half-kilometer outside the wire and wait for the enemy, hell, a squad could have done that. Nate figured the only way for his team to reestablish their confidence was to jump right back in the saddle and pull off riskier operations. They produced heftier rewards and built confidence. It took some reassurance on Nate's part, but his team quickly climbed on board.

After a couple of 'dummy drops' from CAAT, Reaper Two unloaded near their destination. The moon hung low overhead as they methodically cleared a way into the compound. Nate gladly lets the engineer attachments lead the way with their metal detectors, and he marked the cleared areas with infrared chem lights indicating the clear walkways. Until then, he'd taken point in searching for IEDs for his team.

Once inside, they identified three ideal rooms. The engineers inspected the rooms, and one engineer explained he didn't have a good feeling about the room on the far right. A pre-constructed murder hole meant someone had already been there. Regardless of who'd occupied it before, the enemy loved to booby trap and IED rooms, rooftops, and places they believed we could use multiple times. Coincidentally, weeks later another unit occupied the exact compound, and a Marine lost both legs to an IED.

The team cleared and occupied the middle and left rooms, leaving everything else untouched to reduce their signature. To avoid IEDs, they didn't walk anywhere, or touch anything except what was absolutely necessary. Then they went to work knocking holes in the ceilings from inside the rooms. With ladders, they climbed onto the roofs, and Nate kept two men up observing with periscopes while everyone else waited inside.

The sounds of roosters and motorcycle engines filled the early morning air. The snipers on watch didn't wait long, when a few men presented themselves in a target building nearly 350 meters away. Soon, a few more men walking from the south joined them, followed by a few more men arriving on motorcycles. As the men gathered, Signals Intelligence collected intelligence from enemy radio traffic. Just then, Nate noticed a very large, stout individual who obviously wasn't a farmer or sheepherder. He was definitely a fighter, and well built. He may also have been a leader since he directed traffic. When the big guy presented a weapon and an Icom radio, his fate was sealed. Though Afghani's carried weapons, no one but fighters carried radios.

Nate decided to spring the trap and directed six men up on the roof. They prepared to unleash hell with a coordinated shot. Mac used his laser range finder then relayed the distance while suggesting a wind call. During the countdown, Nate aimed center mass at the larger fighter's chest. He wasn't getting away.

The suppressed rifles barely made a sound as the attack started. Nate's target and another man fell from multiple shots, sending the other fighters into a panic. Nate continued rapid-fire, manipulating his rifle's bolt. He tracked a runner and squeezed off a round. He would've been hit, but the lucky bastard stopped as his intended bullet slammed into the wall a few feet in front of him. Surprisingly, the fighters moved about fearlessly. Nate believed they were veteran fighters. They tried hard to find our snipers, taking fire instead of running away. Inevitably, they disappeared after finding the sniper's location.

After a short wait, the fighters sent two men on one moped to probe the sniper lines. They drove by staring at the team only to turn around and pass once more. "These fuckers are gathering intel on us!" said Mac. No one in their right mind drives to the location of a firefight, twice! He was right, Nate gave the word to shoot if they returned. Unfortunately for them, the two returned once more.

"They're coming back!" "Hit'em!" yelled Nate as he grabbed his rifle and climbed onto the roof. Before he set up his gun, the others opened up and knocked both men off their moped. One bled to death from his stomach. The other screamed at the top of his lungs in agony. Nate could barely see his arms and legs moving behind a mound where he'd fallen. Since they were so close to the team, he decided to inspect the bodies for Intel.

Nate grabbed three others and rushed to the downed fighters. As the Marines approached, the man still alive pointed at his stomach, moaning in pain. He appeared to want help, but Nate wanted to inspect the other body first. He found an Icom radio. The other insurgent died before anyone could save him.

The Battalion inquired about the situation, prompting an update from Nate. He reported the events and explained he wanted to leave the bodies in place and try and catch the men's accomplices. He received an 'affirmative' and the men hurried back to their hide. Non-stop traffic flooded the road where the bodies lay, yet not one person looked in the direction of the dead. No one stopped to help; obviously they were bad people.

The bodies lay in place that night, and into the next day. At one point, a stray dog trotted up to the bodies, pissed on both of them, looked up at the snipers on the roof, and continued down the road. Everyone laughed uncontrollably. Later, ANA soldiers finally recovered the bodies.

That night, a mounted patrol extracted the team. Days later, the PB Commander congratulated Nate and his team. One of the dead was a Taliban commander, the other a bomb maker.

A wave of relief swept over Nate, having been able to kill the enemy and return safely. He was in a tough position between motivating his men, and attacking the enemy. The mission could have been a tipping point, considering some of his teammates' mental state. Had they taken another casualty from IEDs, resistance to future missions would have been greater.

Bodies at Griffin

After a long and intense week of fighting near Deh Karez, Reaper Two trucked back to Griffin. While gone, daily RPG and machine gun attacks plagued the base at sundown all week. My men made it a personal mission to re-establish dominance and settle the dirt squirrel rebellion.

The team arrived and dropped gear in their living quarters, a few mud huts infested with fleas, then visited the Intel hooch for an update. The Team Leaders, Nate, and Mac talked with the Signals Intel Team. They learned the enemy had moved within a few hundred meters, and shot at the Sentries and patrols. Normally there was one radio call sign for the man who counted the number of Marines or patrols leaving the base. Now there were seven. Business had picked up. The Marines also found more IEDs than usual. For some reason, enemy activity spiked, and Nate knew why.

The Base Commander, a Lieutenant, refused to let his Marines return fire for fear of hitting civilians or damaging property. That fat piece of shit was just the kind of officer the Marine Corps was now keeping around. He prioritized his career over war fighting, and the shit bag was later promoted to Captain and retained. But I digress.
That day, a patrol prepared to leave, and Nate took to the elevated post to cover the men. While he and his partner scanned for targets, the Signals Intel Marine next to him waited to intercept radio traffic. His other two-man sniper team did the same on the opposite side of the base.

The squad departed, and enemy radio traffic revealed the patrol was under observation. Another enemy transmission intercepted reported. "We're in position and ready to do the work on the infidels." The thick vegetation hid the enemy firing positions, so the team shifted their focus to the enemy's eyes and ears, the Observers. Without them, the attack would probably falter, causing the enemy to retreat after a few shots.

Shortly after, the squad took fire, pinning them down from two PKM's positioned across the Wadi. Concurrently, enemy radio traffic revealed multiple individuals coordinating fire on the squad. One enemy fighter, supposedly from Europe, stood out by his accent. Three others talked of gathering weapons and maneuver on the squad. By then, Nate and his snipers found and identified the Observers.

Across the village, they ID'd a few men who appeared to be directing the action. One wore a very different set of clothing and walked down a trail in a field with a shovel over his left shoulder. Most wouldn't have given him a second look, but our snipers noticed his attempt to conceal a radio in his right hand. The antenna sticking out of his sleeve was a dead giveaway. He quickly jogged down the path for a better vantage point, unknowingly running directly toward the snipers. He was 450 meters from Mac and Grayson when they engaged with the M110 Semi-Auto Sniper System and a burst of M240 machine gun fire. Their barrage peppered the man's stomach and legs, and as he fell, Nate put a round square through his chest. As he lay dying, Justin put a .50 caliber round from the SASR through his head, finishing him off.

The team then turned their attention to the other fighters. Within seconds, Nate identified two men 500 meters away. They peered out of a wheat field next to where the PKM muzzle flash originated. Nate quickly adjusted his scope and with one round, removed a fighter's brain from his head with surgical precision. Immediately, the enemy shooting ceased, as the snipers searched for other targets. After an hour, with nothing significant to report, the teams moved to the COC to debrief the engagement and prepare their reports.

Nate and Mac typed away, when post three, by the front gate, called to say locals were approaching with two bodies. The snipers finished their reports, and Nate anxiously approached the front gate to examine and confirm the bodies were indeed the insurgents the team had killed. Every time locals brought in bodies of dead Taliban, Nate donned a pair of blue medical gloves and examined the terminal ballistic effects on the body. After a few examinations, the locals looked at him very cautiously and quickly figured out that he was not a doctor or a corpsman. He was a monster of a man at 6'2" and a steely-eyed killer built like a machine, with full sleeve tattoos.

After checking the bodies, Nate returned to the team room with information. The enemy observer had taken multiple hits in the torso with half his head removed. Unbelievably, the fighter Nate shot took a round two inches above his left eye but was somehow still alive! The Lieutenant called for a medevac and flew the animal to the nearest medical facility. He died in flight.

Shortly after that, the Lieutenant frantically confronted Nate, "I knew that guy!" he said with tears, talking about the man that Nate shot in the face. "Are you serious?" replied Nate. It shocked him that the officer would consider the fighter a friend after he attacked his Marines. His priorities were wrong. Either way, after that engagement, the PB was never directly attacked again while the 3/2 Ghosts were there.

11 THE DAY OF INFAMY

The Day

The stars aligned near the end of July, as Dep, Reaper Four, and I prepared to go south from 7171 to kill more bad guys. We gathered for a mission originally planned for the west side of a Wadi. It was planned to take place near some ruins, but the hide was untenable, and the mission scrapped. It would prove to be a good decision. Intel indicated there was an enemy command and control cell and an IED manufacturing area on the east side of the Wadi. It was near the village of Sandalah, just above Musalamani, a known Taliban headquarters, training, and IED manufacturing site.

Intelligence indicated there were approximately fifty to one hundred insurgents occupying the area we were now planned to occupy. They further indicated the insurgent leadership there oversaw the manufacturing of the majority of IEDs in the Musa Quelah District. That meant these men were directly responsible for the deaths and maiming of the Marines and Afghani's in our Battalion's area from IEDs. Even more, they composed the bombs that killed and maimed our Marine brothers.

A full intel dump unveiled plenty more information. We learned the enemy employed an AGS-17 (fully Automatic Grenade Launcher) along with multiple heavy and light machine guns. The insurgent command cell frequented different compounds in the central area. Our HUMINT (Human Intelligence Team) indicated that Pakistani Advisors from the Haqqani terrorist network, a Taliban ally, and perhaps the ISI (Inter-Services Intelligence) or Pakistani Intelligence had been assisting the Taliban there.

With our initial mission aborted, we quickly planned another one. We'd ambush their command cell on the Northern side of Sandalah. Our numbers were stacked for this mission. Our sniper team brought multiple attachments for different purposes: HUMINT for gathering intel, Engineers for disposing IEDs and clearing routes, SIGINT for monitoring enemy radio traffic, Grunts for security, and a JTAC for calling in close air support. We held the reins on this pony and would be steering, but having the enablers along felt good and increased our confidence.

We departed after dusk and patrolled south along the Wadi. Eventually Boss, Reaper Four's Assistant Team Leader, led us into the dark Musa Quelah Wadi. As much as possible we moved in water since the handmade IEDs malfunctioned more when wet. To say we had backup was an understatement. We had a section of tanks and a mounted Quick React Force staged to the north, plus supporting arms were a call away as we moved in. We also had air support on call throughout the mission. The enemy didn't know it, but we were about to bring the fight right into their living room.

We traveled five and a half kilometers through the heart of enemy territory, bypassing enemy observation points and fighting positions, and navigating IED belts that acted as their defensive perimeters. After finally reaching our hide, a compound, three hours later, our seventeen-man element breathed a sigh of relief, no IEDs went boom. It didn't surprise me, with Boss leading us through the shadows of the Wadi we made it safely.

Boss' was Rob's right-hand man. He may not have known it, but Rob, Reaper Four's leader, had slowly passed the reigns to him, designating more responsibility to him with every mission. Rob trusted he'd make an excellent team leader once he passed Sniper School. He had traits in him that Rob also had. He was a hunter at heart and ready to fight. He'd also deployed to this area already, and picked up on the slightest ground disturbances, making him an excellent point man.

Outside the compound, we searched for IEDs before making entry and splitting up into a security element and a clearing element. After clearing and sweeping, we found a small family made up of mostly women, but a few older men, in the buildings. We decided on using an unoccupied adjoining compound the family reported as being empty. To gather information, we left a detachment of Intel guys and a small security element with the locals. From the number of beds and amount of equipment found in the other compounds, it appeared enemy fighters had been there. We found spent AGS-17 casings, a chest harness for carrying magazines, and small amounts of ammunition. Rob suspected they used the compounds to bed down for mid-day resting.

By 0600, the next morning, we were ready. While Intel probed the locals in the adjoining compound, we held three primary observation posts. Engineers and EOD attachments set charges in the walls to make loopholes when the speakers blasted the morning prayers. Prayer call began as usual, but for some reason it lingered longer and sounded much more intense. Rob quizzed the interpreter, who explained the prayers were calls for 'death to the infidels' and 'death to America!' Shortly after, Rob learned enemy radio transmissions stated "The work is ready, send the men to work." We knew then that our day was about to begin.

At 0630, a local man entered the compound from a side door to the east. When he saw us, he panicked and attacked a Marine, which nearly compromised our position. The crazy old coot got his ass whupped for his trouble and became very compliant and quiet once he hit the floor like a limp rag. Derek, the Marine he'd attacked, dragged the critter to our Corpsman for a quick exam, before returning to his security position.

At 0700, Aerostat, a gigantic blimp with a million dollar camera, spotted an approaching enemy machine gun team and warned us. Three insurgents walked together; two carried AKs, ammo, and communications equipment, and one, a juvenile about eight or nine years old, packed food and water. Behind them walked a very well-dressed larger man carrying a PKM medium machine gun. He looked to be Pakistani, based on his facial characteristics and body type.

Atop his roof, Rob crouched below a three-foot wall and used a periscope to watch the team while coordinating the attack. We passed hand and arm signals and double-checked the DOPE on our rifles. We needed first round hits. The insurgents talked among themselves, unaware, with every step; they were nearer to death. At twenty-five meters, on Rob's cue, he and Rat, the Marine behind the M240 machine gun, blasted the first few while Boss and I targeted the PKM gunner with our M40A5 sniper rifles. Rob opted for his M4 rather than his bolt gun, simply because they were so close, and his M4 was capable of full-auto. When the shooting started, the men were so close Rob could smell them. He engaged the first two by pumping rounds into each. They were mincemeat from the 5.56mm and 7.62 mm rounds. We all turned our sights to the last man, who fell and didn't move.

Rob hadn't noticed at first, but the boy sat next to a body. His young, angry face indicated his intentions, and he reached for the AK. Rob waited his sights on the boy's chest. If he intended on killing one of us, regardless of his age, he would die. Sure enough, he grabbed the weapon, flipped it off safe, and chicken winged the butt stock under his arm to stabilize the gun when firing, but Rob didn't give him the chance. His first round landed center mass into his chest, and the second went through the boy's collarbone.

Although seemingly brutal, Rob's actions were justified. Teaching children to kill infidels was a repercussion of the enemy's religiosity. The psychological effect of shooting the boy hadn't even crossed Rob's mind, in fact, his perspective expressed our collective thoughts on the matter. We didn't care who the enemy was; if they wanted to fight, we were going to kill them. We had to become emotionless, almost robotic. Rob didn't see a young boy; he saw a hostile or non-hostile person.

Thus began an action-filled three-hour engagement. We completely surprised the enemy. They had no idea where we were or how they woke up with us in their back yard undetected. We'd set up the ideal scenario for killing a lot of bad guys.

Shortly after our initial action, Boss' M203 misfired, launching a 40mm grenade straight up into the air. It took a split second for us to process the possibility of its dropping right on top of us. We all dove for cover. In the process, I managed to fall off of a seven-foot roof and almost broke my leg. Lucky for me, my head bounced off the wall on the way down, breaking my fall. Most importantly, I saved my rifle and scope from damage!

The day wore on and Clay, a man deadly accurate and fast with his .50 caliber SASR, perfectly dispatching an insurgent 1,700 meters to the north, across the Wadi and behind some ruins. Another one of my snipers, Chaps, and our EOD tech, Jake, shot fighters in a tree line, hiding in trenches to the southwest 200 meters away. Suddenly, our engineer, Ty, noticed the boy Rob shot was alive and moving. Ty stripped out of his PPE (Personal Protective Equipment) and sprinted to him. He grabbed the boy carrying him into the compound.

Our Corpsmen stabilized the kid and made him as comfortable as possible, even though the boy screamed at them, calling them infidels. That was the difference between the enemy and us. If they captured on of us, our heads would have been sawed off by now. We knew saving the little shit stain was the right thing to do. Most of us had kids of our own. We also figured he'd be full of intelligence information if we could get him back to the rear for processing. We later discovered the boy attended a local madrasa that taught children weapons and tactics. Weeks later, when he was out of the hospital and released to his family, he returned to be a spotter for the Taliban.

The firefight was sporadic for another hour or so. I made a nice shot on a 'mover' at 630 meters. It was a spectacular shot, but it took me a round to get on target. Those fuckers run fast, and while wearing sandals too! It started when I caught sight of an insurgent carrying a radio and weapon, moving to and from the buildings below. He was obviously trying to find us.

My first opportunity for a shot came when he stopped near a house. Instead of dialing in my scope, I offset my optics and let one fly. The round landed high above him and skipped across the rooftop parapet. Shit, I missed! I quickly adjusted as the fighter moved out of view. I patiently waited for another opportunity and found it when he moved back to his original position. I made the most of the opportunity by putting a bullet through the side of his head. He was moving right to left, and between buildings and trees.

Amidst the action, Battalion requested we recover as many bodies as possible. Considering we were in the midst of a firefight, and surrounded by insurgents no less, the request was asinine. I said no, it wasn't worth the risk, and told them we'd try to recover weapons instead. Against my better judgment, I allowed Dep and Rob to run from our hide, under covering fire, to gather the PKM machine gun, AK-47, Icom radio, and ammunition from the dirt squirrels.

The fighting resumed for what seemed like an eternity, but in actuality lasted only another thirty minutes. That's when Battalion called back. They ordered me to collect and retrieve the three closest bodies. The command was completely unfitting for a sniper mission. We never recovered bodies. We took pictures and gathered intel, but never collected bodies. That duty usually fell to the line companies or CAAT. I'd never been asked to retrieve bodies before. Doing so went against sniper doctrine and put us at an unnecessary risk. I looked at Rob saying, "What the fuck, dude?" He shook his head. We agreed they were going to get us killed.

Before sending the Afghani's to recover the bodies, the Forward Air Controller requested a Harriers fly-by as a show of force. They swooped in low, popping flares and eardrums as the roar of their engines rattled the valley. With the Harrier's gone, the two Afghani's with their wheelbarrow left to fetch the bodies. We provided over-watch and cover fire as they retrieved the dead and returned to our compound.

Shortly after enemy radio traffic indicated the AGS-17, they'd used was stashed in a nearby compound to our south. That particular weapon was a thorn in our side. It had been used to attack our patrols and base, and likely used against Reaper One and Three at Salaam Bazaar. Probably even used to pin down Reaper Five a month prior. Capturing or destroying the AGS-17 would be a huge blow to the insurgents, since replacing it would be difficult.

Once again, Battalion demanded we move out, this time to find the heavy machine gun. I understood wanting to capture the weapon, but being on the ground up close and personal with the enemy, we knew there was no solid intel. We had no ID'd location, which made searching for it an unnecessary and high risk. IEDs infested the area, plus we hadn't completely located all enemy locations. Either way, Dep, and Rob gathered a handful of men and went on a wild goose chase. They cleared three or four compounds to our immediate south and found nothing but more insurgents and enemy supplies.

While clearing the compounds, they managed to flush out a handful of squirters and push them east, straight into our sights. At first, they hid behind women and children, once clear, we put them down as well. Jake picked some off with his DMR (Designated Marksman Rifle) a Springfield M14 while another Marine finished got some with a burst from his M240 machine gun.

Before long, Dep, Rob, and the others returned safely to our location. Although they didn't purposely choose to, they revealed our position to the insurgents. Finding us was the enemy's rally cry, because insurgents crawled out of the woodwork ready to fight. One group maneuvered a machine gun team into a compound to our south and began making loopholes to fire from. Derek, an attachment from Kilo Company, killed the men creating the loopholes by demolishing their position with an AT4 rocket, followed by a machine gun barrage from another Marine.

When the fighting cooled down, tanks and QRF vehicles moved into the Wadi to our west to cover our movement and extraction. Once there, they were exposed to the enemy's PKM machine guns that idiotically targeted the hulking tanks, which answered with 7.62mm Coax and .50 caliber machine gun fires. Their rounds cut down insurgents and a good portion of the vegetation around them.

To our dismay, the tanks couldn't close more than a couple hundred yards from us because of the trench systems. Still, having them nearby was reassuring. Their bold presence stopped the enemy fire, and we began extracting from the compound to the vehicles in the Wadi. Soon, only five of us were left in the compound.

At that moment, a strange thing happened. Though we were exhausted from fighting all day, the enemy bodies before us rejuvenated our spirits. They also presented the opportunity for revenge. Maybe it was the toll of daily combat, or maybe we'd become desensitized to death, I'm not sure. Standing there in a brief silence, knowing the men laying dead our feet were responsible for inflicting pain and misery on our fellow Marines, I felt a surge of anger deep in my bones. They had taken the life of a man whom I considered a brother. They'd also gathered his mutilated body parts and hung them in a tree for us to find. I stood burning inside.

Someone jokingly said, "Piss on these assholes!" The joke died almost instantly, and we couldn't help ourselves. Hell, urinating on them still showed more respect for their dead than they showed for ours. In an instant, we baptized the dead insurgents with fluid from our bladders.

The incident lasted less than two minutes. Later, when asked why we did it, Dep said it best. "Killing these assholes simply wasn't enough." My explanation is straightforward. Imagine someone brutally murdering and mutilating your brothers, then audaciously hanging their body parts from trees for the world to see. These same individuals produced bombs that wantonly murder and maimed numerous coalition and civilian personnel. Most importantly, these same people constantly try killing you every day! Ask yourself, what the fuck would you do if you could get your hands on them? These guys were directly responsible for the deaths of Mark and Adam and all other Marines lost in the Musa Quelah District.

For Rob, humiliating them felt instinctual, like a warrior's ultimate display of victory in the game of combat. Although ours was a more subtle form of Victor's actions, which is something that come down since the dawn of man. After all, when it boils down to it, we won, and the prize was our lives. Unless you've experienced it, the feeling can never be explained nor understood.

Back in the compound, we learned the insurgents' identities. One was a Pakistani cell leader known as 'Q', and the others were his Afghan minions. Before departing, we directed two locals to haul the dead terrorist scum, with wheelbarrows, to the tanks and load them on top.

After securing the bodies, recovering the weapons and equipment, and ensuring our men were all accounted for, we realized there wasn't enough room on the trucks for all of us. We asked the tanks for a ride. Their Captain agreed, and we climbed aboard and were off.

Displaying the dead insurgents atop the tanks sent a strong message to the enemy and the locals. We were the lions, the victors. Riding on top the tanks, despite the stench of stinking bodies, felt great, how the Mongols must have felt riding their horses after a hard fought battle. It was all good until we stopped to wait for a medevac bird for the boy Dac had saved. We sat on the tanks, waiting, in the heat next to the decaying bodies; the stench grew to instant barf levels.

After crushing the enemy and evacuating the boy, we were welcomed back to the Battalion Command Post like conquering heroes. Dep and I delivered the bodies and weapons to the Battalion's Executive Officer. He'd watched the fighting from the Battalion's COC via surveillance assets. Rob, aware that our Battalion Operations Officer wanted a confiscated PKM machine gun, left a post-it note on the butt stock of the one we'd captured. It read, "To the Ops-O, (smiley face), signed Reaper Four."

Overall, the day couldn't have been better. We killed twelve insurgents and struck a decisive blow to the terrorists' ability to produce IEDs. We'd kicked some serious ass. Feeling like Victors didn't last long. In spite of what we'd just been through, a First Sergeant confronted us for being out of uniform regulations. Seems our sleeves weren't 'rolled' properly. Funny, he didn't say anything about the blood caked on our skin and clothes.

12 SNIPER OPERATIONS

Shir Ghazy

At the end of July, Dep and I traveled to COP Shir Ghazy to run missions with Reaper Three. After they dropped JDAMs in Salaam Bazaar, accidentally killing civilians along with enemy machine gun teams, Phil stepped down as the Team Leader. As a result Caleb was promoted, so I wanted to observe his first mission. Dep and I tagged along for fun.

We patrolled east of the village and Wadi to a hide we'd surveyed a few days prior. Captain W, the Battalion Air Officer, was our special guest for the mission. He'd call in air support if needed, but I received personal orders from the Operations Officer to ensure his safe return. That said, we placed him between Dep and me the entire time.

In the compound, we decided the best method to observe the area was digging through the mortared walls, rather than exposing ourselves above them. I helped another Marine dig three feet through the shit-infested mortar. Digging through the rotten walls proved more painful and tiresome than I'd imagined.

At 0630, an infantry squad patrolled south, and we immediately spotted people moving to the west and south, inside a village. On our roof, two snipers identified insurgents and dropped them. It took seven rounds to put one man down. As the action happened, I was fuming. I'd spent all that time and effort digging shit-infested mortar only to not have a view. Damn! Shortly after the action, we extracted with a CAAT Section from Weapons Company before the bad guys located us.

Days later, we were in the Wadi again, on foot, heading toward a hide further into enemy territory. The compound hide site we targeted sat on the west side of the Wadi, south of the village, on a terraced field. Once again, I helped build a loophole through an extremely thick wall. Done, the same two snipers teamed up against an insurgent from the rooftop while a squad patrolled to our north. The insurgents were unaware of our position, until Phil, the former Team Leader, unleashed the M107 SASR .50 caliber rifle on another two insurgents to the north. They killed one for sure and possibly the other. After the SASR went off like a cannon, insurgents immediately located us, and enemy radio traffic indicated insurgents were maneuvering rockets, mortars, machine guns, and reinforcements to attack us. Their leader proclaimed no one would leave the compound alive. We contacted QRF for extract, and our engineers used demolition charges to blow a hole in the compound walls for us to move through. Otherwise, we risked injury from IEDs, had we traversed the compound gates and openings.

Soon our QRF, CAAT Black, were en-route. Our engineers rigged charges on the east side of the compound, as CAAT moved closer, they popped smoke and detonated the breaching charges creating a smoked filled gap. Our team ran to the trucks in pairs. After ensuring all our Marines were on board, Dep and I climbed in.

As we pulled away, mortars and rockets screamed in, exploding around us. A Marine in the turret yelled, "What was that?" as an RPG swooshed overhead. "It was an RPG! Shoot back!" I laughed out loud as I said it. Laughter, really is the best medicine. After the RPG, it didn't take long for our guys from CAAT to haul ass and get us back to COP Shir Ghazy.

Operation Kill Joy

Battalion leadership became enamored with our sniper platoon's success and thirsted for more blood. More importantly, they relished in the praise of my men's success from higher commands, particularly Division and MEF (Marine Expeditionary Force). Based on their desire for more attention and our platoon's staggering achievements thus far, I was given the nod to plan and execute regimental approved battalion level scout/sniper missions. The idea was contrary to typical sniper doctrine, pertaining to sniper employment. Normally snipers support other units or a main effort, this time, the scout/sniper platoon and support teams would be the main effort and focus of operations.

Our immediate priority shifted to disrupting enemy actions. For the first mission, our focal point became an area to our east, specifically a Wadi running northeast to the southwest that served as an enemy personnel and logistics corridor. We knew the villages there were enemy assembly areas, harbor locations for transient fighters and key personnel. We planned to incorporate three sniper teams reinforced with EOD, engineers, intelligence assets, a mounted QRF and a section of tanks in support. We also had armed ISR (Intelligence, Surveillance, Reconnaissance, typically unmanned aerial vehicles in the air and fixed and rotary wing support on station. Suffice to say, with plenty of back-ups, we were eager to infiltrate the area simultaneously from different directions.

As always, we departed well after dark, moving five to six kilometers on foot. I traveled with Reaper Two, and, along with Reaper Five, we navigated from the north on ground saturated with IEDs and protected by numerous fighters. Being with Reaper Two put me in a central location where I could best control the teams, maintain situational awareness, and observe the battlefield. Dep fell in with Reaper Five and made liaison with a Section of tanks. I kept

Dag, the JTAC with me since our position would be optimal for him to call in support from our air assets. Rob led Reaper Four from the Southwest. Our two teams patrolled across the barren high desert and into position. As we dropped into the valley, Reaper Five followed the ridge north to an abandoned compound while we moved south to our hide site. It was around 0230, when all three teams reached our final positions.

Among us, the clearing team made entry first, as rehearsed, then the security and overwatch team took up positions around the perimeter and on the rooftops. As for me, I made it to a rooftop and planted my hand on a hornet's nest burrowed in the mud walls. The giant Japanese hornets swarmed out, heading directly up my sleeve, stinging the shit out of me. I wanted to scream, but couldn't. I bit down on my lip as hard as I could and let out a deep breath. Believe me, it fuckin' hurt!

Once the compound and living quarters cleared and deemed safe from IEDs, we set up positions behind the parapets and domes. Our positions allowed us to focus the majority of our observation to the east and northeast covering a good portion of the village across the Wadi. We had good reason to believe that midlevel leaders stayed there.

While establishing observation positions, a few Marines made comms with the battalion command and control cell positioned in the desert a couple kilometers to our west. With all teams in position, we notified higher and settled in for what was supposed to be a relatively short mission. The optimal word in that is 'relatively,' because it turned out to be anything but short.

Around 0700, Nate spotted a growing mass of MAM's (Military Aged Males) on a hilltop 1100 meters to our east-northeast and 1500 meters directly west of Reaper Five's position. We counted approximately fifteen armed insurgents carrying assorted Soviet-style automatic and crew served weapons, plus handheld radios.

We decided an air strike would be the best attack, so Dag, our JTAC, worked to request a mission. From our vantage point on the rooftop, there were no civilians or friendlies anywhere near the insurgents. However, our request was denied. According to Battalion, they found what appeared to be a herd of sheep on the side of the hill that we couldn't observe. The Battalion Commander denied the airstrike, fearing collateral damage with the sheep and sheepherders. We tried pressing the issue but received a strict rebuttal.

Once the air strike was denied, we requested artillery. Again, Dag worked a fire mission requesting GPS guided munitions or HIMMARS. Once again, we were swiftly denied. Our dickhead Battalion Commander was apparently aggravated at us for not initiating the ambush with sniper fire, as briefed before the mission. God forbid we thought on our own and adapted to the situation. We missed the opportunity to kill the enemy. All I could think was 'Thanks,

Sir, you fucking moron. We could have eliminated the whole lot of them without giving away our position to the enemy.'

While we argued with higher about the use of supporting arms, Rob's team down south held a strong position in a compound atop a cliff. They observed insurgents moving within a couple hundred meters of their hide. Since it was quite obvious to everyone on the ground that Battalion would screw us on the use of supporting arms, I gave Rob the nod to initiate the ambush and engage his targets. They opened fire with suppressed weapons on six to seven men, quickly displacing two. After, they immediately noticed an enemy machine gun team moving to a position behind a loophole in a wall a couple hundred meters away. My snipers killed them with an AT4 rocket.

When Reaper Four engaged and ambushed the insurgents to the south, the militants on the hill stood up to assess the situation. They not only exposed themselves to us, we intercepted their conversations, prompting us to attack. Nate, Mac, and I adjusted our scopes. Grayson manned the M240 machine gun, and we all fired opened fire. A younger man with a weapon stood and ran, as I placed a lead on him and squeezed the trigger. I watched him stumble and fall behind the crest of the hill. Reaper   Five opened up with the SASR from their northern position. Later on in the firefight, Nate spotted a small white truck collect the younger insurgent's body, as well as a handful of other dead.

Though still early, the fighting and our day were far from over. Just as we predicted, the enemy began swarming from the villages just as the damned hornets had swarmed up my arm. But, we held the advantage. They were confused and didn't know where we were. Our use of multiple hides and suppressed weapons had achieved tactical surprise. An insurgent radio transmission explained everything. "The ghosts are everywhere; they're killing us all!" We were 'the Ghosts,' men who unexpectedly struck from nowhere and moved unseen in the darkness. The nickname started from Reaper Four in the southern part of our AO but in time moved throughout the entire area. Up north, insurgents referred to my snipers as the Sky People, who struck like lightning from the hill tops.' The enemy knew our capabilities and our reputation. They feared us more than anything else the battalion could throw at them.

As insurgents rushed in reinforcements and evacuate their combatants, we picked off targets of opportunity as they appeared. The majority of them arrived on their Frankenstein motorcycles that we called 'Helmand Davidson's.' The insurgents carried weapons and radios as they moved into position to engage us. For us, it was easy picking. Grayson hit them with a burst of M240 fire, and we finished them off with precision rifle fire. Reaper Two and I killed four this way. One of the insurgents was a very tough bastard or maybe high as a kite on opium. He wouldn't stay down. He took a few shots from all of us. I hit him with a gut shot and a double lung shot. Mac and Nate put a couple into him as well before he went down for good. It was like a deadly game of whack-a-mole, waiting for him to pop up for us to put him back down.

Down south, Rob's team was also having success. They shot reinforcements, and squirters fleeing from the battle. They also coordinated with tanks to blast fighters shooting from murder holes. Rob found it a very sniper friendly environment and enjoyed picking off the fighters as they maneuvered on his team. The insurgents were blocked, by either the terrain or had to move across the open ground, giving his team the advantage. Rob's personal goal was killing as many seasoned fighters as possible. The new fighters died quickly; the savvy veterans were more difficult to track down, or played the game well enough to survive. Their game was knowingly using our Rules of Engagement against us. They did it well.

A long day turned into a very long day. We traded lead with the enemy all morning. At noon, Nate located a group of men sneaking around a wall 975 meters to our south, southeast. We both focused our weapons on them; Nate shot, tagging one. When he fell, his buddy stopped in his tracks. "Ya see him," asked Nate just as I shot. "He'a right about there?" I answered. Nate chuckled as the asshole doubled over and fell to the ground for keeps.

Right then, our EOD tech got hit but not by bullets, but a swarm of those pissed off giant Japanese hornets. No big deal right? Wrong. He swelled up like a freakin' balloon! I thought we'd have to medevac him, which would have been interesting, considering we were under fire in the middle of bad mans land. I gotta' give him credit though, Doc hooked him up with a couple injections, and he refused to let me call in a bird for him. Instead, he propped himself up and held security on the southern entrance to the compound. Later, I was scolded for my decision of not bringing a bird in for him, but fuck it, he was okay.

At around two in the afternoon, the fighting slowed down a bit. A good thing, since we were all running low on ammo, and the majority of our attachments badly needed water. Meanwhile, Battalion demanded we drive on though we'd already killed fifteen confirmed and another handful of possibles. I thought we should move out, but they wanted more, more, and more. More blood, more recognition, and at any cost, it seemed.

Their pressure forced us to hold our position well past our scheduled extract. I had nothing to do except coordinate a resupply of water and ammo for Rob's team in the south and consolidate Reaper Two at Reaper Five's position to the north. I radioed higher and requested a section of mounted vehicles to close on Reaper Two's position, allowing us to push north under their protection, and recover the resupply for Rob's team.

It wasn't long, and Rob's team received their water, ammo, and chow by a mounted squad from Kilo Company. They kicked out the items, then split because the fighting was now rampant. The snipers continually fought off intermittent attacks by probing insurgents. Amidst the chaos, Rob noticed a subtle, yet familiar transformation happening in his younger Marines. It occurred to him that war slowly cooked their minds. Their high school aura was all but gone, replaced by the addictive bloodlust that only combat adrenaline produces. Rob was proud of them, yet sadly sympathetic because now, nothing but more combat can satisfy their new addiction. They might try replacing it with drugs or alcohol, but nothing will ever come close to combat adrenaline.

Finally, after a long day of fighting, our extract vehicles arrived in a field north of our position. We popped smoke and loaded the armored MRAPs and Seven Tons. As we began moving north, we met up with Josh and everyone at Reaper Five's position. As we did, We took intense machine gun fire from the north and northeast.

13 COMING HOME

On our way out of the country, my platoon and I were treated to a private breakfast with the Commandant and Sergeant Major of the Marine Corps. The highest ranking officer and enlisted man in the Corps. After the platoon's many successes and rave reviews by the Commanding Generals of II MEF and CentCom, the Commandant, and Sergeant Major wanted to personally thank us for our accomplishments, hard work, and dedication.

The Commandant had a special meal prepared, and an area set aside for us to join him at Camp Leatherneck. He thanked us for our service and handed each of our men a challenge coin. The Sergeant Major followed suit and did the same. The men found the attention and recognition pretty amazing. In some small way, it reinforced the Marine

Corps' gratitude for a job well done above and beyond what most had expected.

Following the meal, our platoon packed up and headed out to their flights to Manass Air Base in Kyrgyzstan. I had to stay back with the Battalion Command and Staff for a meeting with the Commander of the JSOC Task Force. It appeared we'd caught their attention as well. The day after the men departed, I sat down with an individual at II MEF Headquarters, and he began asking questions. He was particularly interested in how we were able to target and eliminate so many insurgents and High Valued Targets.

I'm not sure exactly what he was expecting or if he thought there was some great new tactic I could share? I remember him asking, "So how did you kill so many of them? I mean how did you get a positive ID on the targets and engage them so efficiently?" My response was quite simple. "Sir, when y'all go in, you use choppers and telegraph to everyone you're coming. We walk; we simply walk in and wait and wait and wait, and then we kill them."

Shortly after this conversation, we were all on our way home. The guys made it home a few days ahead of me, but that's alright; there was a whole group of folks there to meet them! When you come home, there are worlds of emotions that flood you. You're overjoyed to be home and be with your family, but at the same time you miss the drive and exhilaration and camaraderie that you enjoyed over there. For me, I was grateful to be with my wife and kids again, but part of me missed the war. It happened every time I've come home, and this time was no different. I think a part of me will always miss being there, whether it's Iraq or Afghanistan. And a part of me was left over there and will never come home again.

Soon though, life settled into a routine, and the inevitable orders and changes to the unit and platoon began. I cross decked to 1st Battalion 8th Marines to go back over in January of 2012. The majority of the senior guys in our platoon began to execute orders to other units or process out of the Corps. It's always hectic when a unit returns from post-deployment leave. The command changes and the people move in and out, as the focus shifts to the next work up and deployment.

It was during this time after I'd transferred units, that I got 'the call'. It was a Thursday morning in January 2012, just days before I was heading back over to Afghanistan with 1/8. I received 'the call' that would change my life forever. Pete called me and told me to look up a URL and watch a video. He said it was 'leaked', and I needed to see what was happening.

I followed the URL to TMZ, and watched a video of myself, two other Marines from my platoon, and one security attachment urinating on enemy combatants on our mission south of the pyramids. The video was leaked to the media and this simple act of ignorance and selfishness, on one man's part, opened up a whirlwind that destroyed so many lives and careers. So many people involved, both directly and indirectly in the video and the mission, were forever branded. I hope karma kicks that dude's ass.

That Friday, six hours prior to getting on a bird and going back in the fight, I was called to stand before the Battalion Executive Officer of 1/8's office. I was the told to report to the NCIS East office with our Gunny. After Pete's call, I contacted a lawyer, Mr. Gittins, and I knew what to do. I gave the agents my basic information, then told them I refused to wave my rights. They could direct all questions to my legal counsel. I was then, unceremoniously and immediately cut orders to 2d Marine Regiment, where I would wait to learn my fate. Instead of being allowed to go do my job and lead men back into combat to destroy the enemies of my country, I was placed on hold.

While all of this was going on, my marriage was also suffering. The time away, the deployments, and lack of communication over the years had taken its toll. As the battle for my career and the battle in my mind raged, the world around me splintered into tiny pieces. I was physically and emotionally drained, running on empty. During this time, I was given my second back surgery and was put on a Med Board, which was subsequently canceled so I could be court-martialed. The Med Board was reconvened afterward.

In the midst of my turmoil, Doctors said I had serious issues with the dreaded PTSD monster and some TBI from exposure to blasts over the years. They recommended inpatient treatment in a clinic in San Antonio, Texas. While I didn't like the news as the time, but it turned out to be a blessing in disguise. I had so many issues I'd put into the back of my mind that I now knew needed to be addressed. The time as an inpatient allowed me to refocus and determine I was going to achieve victory out of all of this.

It was there I began to write what have become this book. I was able to put my thoughts into words. I knew I must tell the story of my men. I knew people had to know more than just the cheapened version of events portrayed on the news. The truth of our Marines and their stories needed to be told. The American people need to know and understand, in order to win a war, we must be willing to do whatever it takes. The people of America and the political system need to face reality. They need to understand you can't have the politically correct pretty boy façade and the dealer in death who takes the fight to the enemy. You simply can't have both ways.

Writing this book was therapeutic, and it allowed me to begin to process a majority of the things I've seen and done. Some things I will never fully understand and some things just do not need repeating or remembering, and there are some things that will remain a memory only for me and the men that were there. Even though this helped me in gaining insight into myself, unfortunately, it wasn't enough to save my marriage. We separated shortly after my retirement and moved to towns down the road from each other in Tennessee. It seemed like a great place for us to start fresh and still be close enough to raise our amazing children together. I know this experience has been hard on them, but they are amazingly resilient and bring so much joy into my life.

I also didn't allow the US political system to destroy my life. I don't want it to destroy the lives of the men who fought and bled over there either. The Department of Defense and Department of State wanted our heads on a spit, and the USMC's hierarchy was more than willing to oblige. They tried, but at the end of the day, I won; I guess some things just weren't in the cards of the powers that be.

Some of my men fell into depression and searched out drugs and parties. They needed to replace the void left inside them when their so-called brothers and the Corps turned their backs on them. A majority of those young men are still in that place, most still searching for who they are and what their future now holds.

It's been horrible to watch, as these once proud men suffer in silence, feeling rejected. They've been left out in the cold by the same institution that just months before praised them for their selfless sacrifice and willingness to kill the enemy. In all honesty, the only group of people that stood by my men and me, was our fellow scout/snipers, a Brotherhood of shared pain. These men went out of their way to help and defend us, with one exception, Sergeant Major Michael Barrett, then Sergeant Major of the Marine Corps. Sergeant Major Barrett was a former Scout/Sniper Instructor and as it turns out, Uncle Tom extraordinaire! What a piece of shit.

In September of 2013, I was medically retired at the rank of Sergeant. My time in the Marine Corps was over. It was definitely, a bittersweet moment. I was frustrated. They didn't give me the opportunity to finish my twenty years and retire, and finish what I'd started. At the same time, I was glad it was over. Honestly, I didn't want to remain in an organization that would turn its back on its members at the drop of a hat. I wouldn't change my time in or the things I have seen and done. I wouldn't even change pissing on those animals, I just wouldn't video tape it again.

I sincerely hope this book answers some of the questions concerning this event. I also hope this book will give people a small glimpse into the mindset and life of a group of young men who laid it all on the line for their country, their families, and most of all for each other. They were and are some of the best men I've ever known. They are so much more than a 39 second video could ever depict. It's an honor Gentlemen.

Never above you, Never below you, Always beside you. *Semper Fi Brothers*

ABOUT THE AUTHOR

While on his last deployment to Afghanistan with 3rd Battalion 2d Marines in 2011 his Scout Sniper Platoon delivered a devastating toll on the enemy, inflicting well over 300 enemy KIA and numerous other casualties. It was on this deployment is also where the YouTube video was taken. Joe was the leader of the team involved and one of the Marines in the infamous "Marine Urination Video Scandal".

He has now broken his silence in order to ensure his Marines entire stories are told. Stories of his men's courage, sacrifice and heroism that has become unjustly over shadowed by a 39 second video. The men of 3rd Battalion 2d Marines Scout Sniper Platoon deserve for the world to know the rest of their story.

Other Books You Might Enjoy

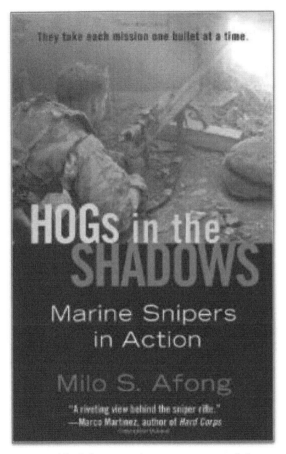

Available on Amazon and in book stores everywhere!

Other Books You Might Enjoy

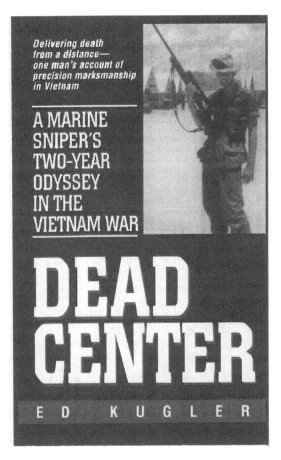

Delivering death from a distance—one man's account of precision marksmanship in Vietnam

A MARINE SNIPER'S TWO-YEAR ODYSSEY IN THE VIETNAM WAR

DEAD CENTER

ED KUGLER

Available on Amazon and in book stores everywhere!

19794664R00130

Made in the USA
Middletown, DE
05 May 2015